T0286799

Cambridge Elements ≡

Elements in the Politics of Development
edited by
Rachel Beatty Riedl
Einaudi Center for International Studies and Cornell University
Ben Ross Schneider
Massachusetts Institute of Technology

Mario Einaudi
CENTER FOR
INTERNATIONAL STUDIES

 MIT CENTER FOR INTERNATIONAL STUDIES

LOCKED OUT OF DEVELOPMENT

Insiders and Outsiders in Arab Capitalism

Steffen Hertog
The London School of Economics and Political Science

 CAMBRIDGE
UNIVERSITY PRESS

Shaftesbury Road, Cambridge CB2 8EA, United Kingdom

One Liberty Plaza, 20th Floor, New York, NY 10006, USA

477 Williamstown Road, Port Melbourne, VIC 3207, Australia

314–321, 3rd Floor, Plot 3, Splendor Forum, Jasola District Centre, New Delhi – 110025, India

103 Penang Road, #05–06/07, Visioncrest Commercial, Singapore 238467

Cambridge University Press is part of Cambridge University Press & Assessment, a department of the University of Cambridge.

We share the University's mission to contribute to society through the pursuit of education, learning and research at the highest international levels of excellence.

www.cambridge.org
Information on this title: www.cambridge.org/9781009045575

DOI: 10.1017/9781009042444

First published 2022

A catalogue record for this publication is available from the British Library.

ISBN 978-1-009-04557-5 Paperback
ISSN 2515-1584 (online)
ISSN 2515-1576 (print)

Additional resources for this publication at www.cambridge.org/hertog.

Locked Out of Development

Insiders and Outsiders in Arab Capitalism

Elements in the Politics of Development

DOI: 10.1017/9781009042444
First published online: December 2022

Steffen Hertog
The London School of Economics and Political Science
Author for correspondence: Steffen Hertog, S.Hertog@lse.ac.uk

Abstract: This Element argues that the low dynamism of low- to mid-income Arab economies is explained with a set of interconnected factors constituting a "segmented market economy." These include an overcommitted and interventionist state with limited fiscal and institutional resources; deep insider–outsider divides among firms and workers that result from and reinforce wide-ranging state intervention; and an equilibrium of low skills and low productivity that results from and reinforces insider–outsider divides. These mutually reinforcing features undermine encompassing cooperation between state, business, and labor. While some of these features are generic to developing countries, others are regionally specific, including the relative importance and historical ambition of the state in the economy and, closely related, the relative size and rigidity of the insider coalitions created through government intervention. Insiders and outsiders exist everywhere, but the divisions are particularly stark, immovable, and consequential in the Arab world.

Keywords: Arab economies, dual markets, insider–outsider, segmentation, varieties of capitalism

ISBNs: 9781009045575 (PB), 9781009042444 (OC)
ISSNs: 2515-1584 (online), 2515-1576 (print)

Contents

1 Introduction: Arab Capitalism   1

2 Historical Roots   14

3 Segmented Market Economies   29

4 Individual Country Outcomes and Alternative Explanations   72

5 Comparative Puzzles and Gaps   77

6 Conclusion   80

References   84

A Further Online Appendix can be accessed at
www.cambridge.org/Hertog

1 Introduction: Arab Capitalism

Among Middle East experts, it is a frequently espoused view – if not received wisdom – that pro-market reforms are the root cause of the social discontent that has driven unrest across the Arab world since 2010 (Achcar 2013; Bogaert 2013; Joya 2017; Kaboub 2013). According to this reading, neoliberal policies have exposed increasing numbers of Arab citizens to the inequality and poverty resulting from unfettered capitalism. This narrative sits uneasily with a number of facts: Most Arab countries continue to employ more citizens in their state apparatus than other countries of comparable income; subsidy systems, while shrinking, have continued to be unusually expansive; and Arab governments continue to intervene deeply in private markets through licensing systems, nontariff trade barriers (NTTBs), and allocation of land and credit. By standard measures, all other major regions of the Global South remain more "neoliberal" than the Arab world.

This Element proposes an alternative explanation for both the socioeconomic frustrations of Arab citizens and, critically, the broader economic development failures of the core Arab world: the problem is not exposure to capitalism per se but the *very uneven* exposure of Arab citizens and firms to markets, rooted in their uneven access to the state's resources and protection. The past decades have seen marketization for some parts of the population – especially younger labor market entrants and small firms consigned to the growing informal economy – yet continued protection and insider privileges for others, be they state employees or larger firms with deep connections to the state apparatus. I argue that deep divisions between insiders and outsiders are the defining dynamic of the political economies of core Arab countries, especially the Arab republics with a deeper legacy of state-directed development. I do not deny that private markets have become more important over time or that the region's old, more inclusive "social contract" has eroded, as has been pointed out by a wide range of authors (Achcar 2013; Bogaert 2013; Devarajan and Ianchovichina 2018; Heydemann 2007; Kaboub 2013; Kandil 2012). Yet this erosion has been happening very unevenly, leading to forms of social exclusion and patterns of economic stagnation that a simple marketization story cannot explain.

As a result, different segments of both labor and capital exist in very different spheres: on the labor market there are millions badly paid but still fundamentally secure lower middle-class bureaucrats. They are emblematic figures in Arab public imagination, immortalized in the 1992 Egyptian black comedy "Terror and Kebab," in which the protagonist, played by Adel Imam, accidentally takes the Mugamma bureaucratic complex at Tahrir Square hostage when his frustration with idle and unresponsive government workers leads to a scuffle and mass panic. While often frustrated, Arab state employees remain shielded from the market, enjoy formal social security, and are extremely secure in their tenure. They are insiders.

While Arab bureaucrats are numerous, there are even more workers in the region's informal sector – the most famous of them Mohamed Bouazizi, the unlicensed Tunisian fruit vendor who set himself on fire on December 17, 2010, after repeated harassment by local police forces (themselves state-employed insiders by this Element's account). Far from secure, informal workers in the Arab world fight a daily battle for economic survival and enjoy even less social safety provision than their peers in other parts of the Global South. They operate in a raw, unregulated private market, and their frustrations were a key driver of the revolutionary fervor unfolding in Tunisia after Bouazizi's dramatic act of protest. They are quintessential outsiders and their outsider status tends to be unusually long-lasting.

A similar story of insiders and outsiders can be told about firms: on the one hand, state elites and institutions protect large firms led by cronies like Egyptian steel magnate Ahmed Ezz or Syrian telecoms, retail and real estate baron Rami Makhlouf. Shielded from competition through mechanisms like discretionary regulation, subsidies, and access to credit, insider firms enjoy unusually deep protection from the market. On the other hand, the vast majority of businesses in the Arab world are small, informal enterprises – grocery stores, repair shops, small-scale construction companies – which are struggling to survive on the unregulated market, let alone grow, as state institutions are at best indifferent and at worst openly hostile to them. As I will argue, the forces keeping outsider firms small and precarious are unusually strong in the Arab world.

While belonging to the same social classes from a macro perspective, insiders and outsiders in the labor market and among capitalists in reality represent very different constituencies, with fundamentally different relationships to the state and often opposed interests. Insider–outsider divides account for key sources of socioeconomic frustration among Arab citizens such as declining social mobility and elite-level cronyism, important drivers of recurrent unrest since 2010.

The deep segmentation of insiders and outsiders is consistent with the low growth and dynamism of Arab economies more broadly. The weak performance of Arab economies over the past decades is hard to overstate and difficult to explain just with excessive pro-market reforms: the region boasts the world's highest unemployment rates, the lowest share of hi-tech goods in manufactured exports, the lowest firm entry rates, and the smallest growth in labor productivity (Arezki et al. 2019; Arezki et al. 2021; Benhassine 2009; European Bank for Reconstruction and Development 2013; Gatti et al. 2013).

Most Arab countries have comparatively institutionalized state apparatuses, have made great strides in providing basic public goods in health and education, and lie in close proximity to European markets – yet seem unable to make effective use of these assets. While my main aim is not to explain the region's growth record, the deep structural divisions of labor and capital documented in this Element are bound to hamper economic development. State-sanctioned segmentation of insiders and outsider in labor markets and private business undermines the dynamism of Arab economies, leads to misallocation of resources, weakens incentives for firms to improve productivity and provide training, and reduces workers' incentives to seek skills. The Arab world's core development problem arguably is persistent dualism rather than unrestrained capitalism.

My argument cuts across several spheres of the economy, and I propose that weaknesses in different spheres reinforce each other. I therefore frame my account in terms of the wider "Varieties of Capitalism" debate, which focuses on capturing such system-wide institutional linkages and complementarities.

I specifically argue that core Arab economies outside of the oil-rich Gulf are regulated by stretched, overcommitted, and interventionist states. Uneven regulation and unbalanced distribution of scarce resources by this state creates deep insider–outsider divides in private sectors and labor markets. These divisions themselves reinforce lopsided state intervention through economic and political feedback loops: insider interests are relatively better organized and recognized by political elites, while the politics of outsiders is typically limited to sporadic outbursts of protest. An equilibrium of low skills and low productivity results from and reinforces these static insider–outsider divides: protected insiders feel little competitive pressures to improve skills or productivity; similarly, as outsiders are unable to effectively compete with insiders, their ability and incentives to invest in skills and productivity are also limited.

The region's social divisions, and the resulting divergence of interests, undermine cooperation and trust between state, business, and labor, hence impeding the negotiation of encompassing reforms or skill system upgrades that could overcome economic dualism. Exclusion of outsiders and low productivity of insiders quite likely contribute to weak diversification and growth outcomes in the region.

Some fundamental parts of this story apply to economies in the Global South in general, notably low government capacity and a segmentation of business and labor into formal and informal markets. Others, however, are regionally specific, including the relative importance and historical ambition of the state in the economy and, closely related, the unusual rigidity of insider–outsider divisions. Insiders and outsiders exist everywhere, but the dividing lines are particularly stark, immovable, and consequential in the Arab world, hence the term "seg-mented market economies" to describe our cases (henceforth SEME).[1]

The formerly "populist" Arab republics Algeria, Egypt, and (pre-civil war) Syria with their deep and ambitious histories of state intervention are closest to this ideal type. Economically somewhat more liberal systems like early repub-lican reformer Tunisia and pro-capitalist monarchies Jordan and Morocco are less perfect fits, as is Yemen, which has been too poor historically to develop the same level of state intervention as its republican peers. Yet in international comparison, even the latter cases stand out more often than not on the inter-linked features discussed in this Element.

The ambition of this Element, like in much of the Varieties of Capitalism (VoC) literature, is both conceptual and explanatory: it first aims to identify the main features of capitalism in key Arab cases to then illustrate how they are causally interlinked through mutually reinforcing mechanisms of insider–outsider segmentation. It proposes that these features of Arab capitalism account for the generally low economic dynamism that the region has seen in terms of job creation, firm creation, and skills formation, and that insider–outsider divides have also shaped socioeconomic frustration, political mobil-ization, and protest over recent decades. Theoretically, the Element extends the political economy of insider–outsider labor markets – much analyzed in the European context – to the developing world, where this socially corrosive phenomenon thus far has mostly been investigated through a purely economic lens.

After an explanation of its case selection and method, the Element outlines the segmented market economies concept in more conceptual detail, followed by an overview of the historical roots of etatism in the Arab world. The subsequent sections investigate the state, labor, firms, and the market for skills. I then discuss whether the harsh economic adjustments that Egypt has under-gone since 2016 presage the trajectory of the wider region and discuss a number of theoretical puzzles and gaps in general comparative political economy that emerge from this Element's arguments.

1.1 Case Selection and Method

This Element deals with seven Arab countries that can be considered "core" members of the region: Algeria, Egypt, Jordan, Morocco, pre-2011 Syria, Tunisia, and pre-2015 Yemen.[2] These have been part of a shared regional

---

[1] I choose SEME to distinguish the concept from Schmidt's "state-influenced market economies" or SMEs, advanced capitalist countries with an interventionist state (Schmidt 2009).

[2] Data on Syria in this Element are from 2010 or just before; data on Yemen are from 2015 or earlier.

space of political competition and ideological diffusion in the post–World War II era in a way that more peripheral members of the Arab League like Djibouti, Mauritania, and Sudan have not been (Choueiri 2000; Kerr 1965; Mufti 1996).

I exclude high-rent countries – the Gulf Cooperation Council (GCC) monarchies and Libya – where hydrocarbons income has created substantially different economic structures.[3] I also do not systematically discuss countries whose economies have been shaped by major, long-term conflicts before the 2010s, like Iraq and Lebanon.[4]

One might criticize the Element for cherry-picking cases. Investigating a limited number of cases that approach a particular ideal type is, however, standard practice in the VoC literature and is difficult to avoid given the relative complexity and limited range of the theories it proposes. Our omission of more peripheral Arab cases is also in line with definitions of the region among international institutions.[5]

Perhaps more important, the case selection in this Element is theoretically motivated by a particular set of historical circumstances that determine the applicability of its model: it only includes countries that engaged in an ambitious state-building project that was directly or indirectly affected by the nationalist and statist ideological competition dominating the region from the 1950s to the 1970s. Aggregate comparative data on the rest of the Middle East and North Africa (MENA) region as well as other world regions as "control groups" are contained in the online appendix (O6).

As we will see, even among our core cases, some fit the model considerably better than others – and it is the ones that pursued the nationalist state-building project the most ardently that show the best fit. Morocco, the most peripheral of my "core" cases in this Element that was least affected by the nationalist and statist wave of the post–World War II era, has the worst fit.

1.2 Existing Literature on MENA Political Economy

Existing literature on the political economy of the Arab region captures some of its development issues, but also fails to describe and explain key features that make the region distinct.

---

[3] The GCC countries have notably been able to absorb a majority of the national workforce in the public sector and rely on a migrant workforce for most private sector jobs. There is little informal employment of citizens, while there is considerable informal employment of foreigners, including in informal foreign-run businesses. Labor markets and private sectors are therefore also segmented, but in very different ways (Hertog 2014; 2021).

[4] Although excluded, pre-2011 Libya and pre-1979 authoritarian-populist Iraq share many of the features of our model.

[5] https://data.worldbank.org/region/middle-east-and-north-africa; www.unescwa.org/about-escwa.

Most prominently, critiques of "neoliberal" economic adjustment across the region rightly point to growing inequality, state withdrawal, and corruption from (imperfect) marketization and privatization as key features of regional economic development since the 1970s (Achcar 2013; King 2009; Mitchell 1999). Yet in international comparison, the Arab world remains the least neoliberal region apart from a small number of socialist holdover countries. State intervention and protection for select sectors and actors remain pervasive, if substantially less so than during the nationalist phase of the 1960s. Recent literature on crony capitalism in the region has shown in great detail that the elite-level insider cartels that have emerged from partial marketization since the 1970s remain rooted in state intervention in licensing, trade protection, and allocation of credit and subsidies. Literature in labor market economics (and original research in this Element) shows that Arab labor markets are not generally market-driven but instead are deeply divided between protected insiders and precarious outsiders – and the precariousness and lack of social safety mechanisms for these outsiders are explained not least with the fact that large-scale resources are devoted to insider privileges in the shape of state employment, regressive subsidy schemes, and contribution-based, state-supported social security. In Arab economies, some face brutal exposure to (often informal) markets but others benefit from unusually deep protection from the market. More generally, as Adly (2020, 9) has pointed out, Arab development failures are as much a problem of distribution as they are a problem of weak production, which the neoliberal narrative has little to say about. This Element focuses on the many ways in which insider–outsider divides undermine the productive capacity of Arab economies.

The focus of other authors on the (neo-)patrimonial nature of Arab capitalism usefully highlights the informal nature of elite-level insider coalitions (Heydemann 2004; King 2009; Schlumberger 2008). I propose, however, that formal rules and institutions can matter at least as much in organizing economic exclusion in the region. Moreover, insider–outsider dynamics also play out on the lower rungs of the labor market, which contains a large and theoretically neglected insider group of formal state employees. This group can be both fiscally and politically as consequential as elite coalitions.

Literature on the decline of corporatist institutions and the broken promises of social progress among Arab regimes rightly points to the erosion of old social contracts (Ehteshami and Murphy 1996; Guazzone and Pioppi 2009; King 2009). Past social guarantees – perhaps most prominently that of state employment for all university graduates – have indeed eroded, the Arab middle classes are falling behind, and social mobility has been declining across the region (Assaad et al. 2021). This literature does, however, not tell us much about the important areas in which insider privileges continue to be upheld, which extend beyond capitalist elites to a well-protected, rather large minority of formal employees – and which often contribute to the declining social mobility of new labor market entrants and their resulting political frustration.

More broadly, existing literature does not engage systematically with linkages between different spheres of the economy like the private sector, the labor market, and the (seldom discussed) skills system. Most authors also focus primarily on within-region differences rather than situating the region in global comparative context (Ayubi 1995; Cammett et al. 2015; Henry and Springborg 2010). In both these regards, a VoC approach holds particular promise. It can help bring the Arab world region back into comparative perspective and make it a source of broader comparative political economy theorizing, which it has largely ceased to be since the 1980s.

1.3 "Varieties of Capitalism" Approaches and the Arab World

The basic premise of VoC is that capitalism is not uniform. Instead, firms and workers in different advanced economies use different formal and informal ways of coordinating economic transactions. The core spheres of coordination in the original, firm-centered VoC formulation by Hall and Soskice are corporate governance and finance, intercompany networks, industrial relations, and skills systems (Hall and Soskice 2001).

Most variants of VoC assume that different features of a given type of capitalism are complementary and reinforce each other through mutually "increasing returns": patterns of exchange in one sphere increase the payoffs to complementary behavior in related spheres. In European "coordinated market economies," for example, cooperative industrial relations between employers and workers result in high job security, which allows education systems to focus on the acquisition of specialized skills – which conversely empower workers in industrial relations negotiations. The longer-term focus of this equilibrium in turn allows banks to provide firms with long-term, "patient" capital, which itself helps firms to focus on long-, rather than short-term profitability – a focus that is more compatible with employment stability and worker interests (Hall and Soskice 2001). Such complementarities keep a system in an equilibrium that privileges certain types of exchange such as short-term, market-based interactions in the case of Anglo-American liberal market economies or long-term, nonmarket based exchanges in the case of coordinated market economies like Germany.

While the original VoC formulation has been much criticized, it has spawned an ongoing search for different types of capitalism not only among advanced countries but also in less developed areas (Feldmann 2019; Nölke et al. 2015; Nölke and Vliegenthart 2009; Schneider 2013; Walter and Zhang 2012).

Although based on a study of Latin American cases, Schneider's account of "hierarchical market economies" (HMEs) comes closest to a full-fledged model of complementary institutions that could apply to developing countries in general. HMEs are characterized by the dominance of diversified, technologically unsophisticated private conglomerates, a strong presence of transnational companies, atomized labor relations and low skills. He argues that these factors and the interactions between them are characterized by nonmarket, *hierarchical* relationships that undermine horizontal coordination, and that there are "negative complementarities" between them, resulting in a low-skills equilibrium that prevents Latin America from catching up with advanced countries. The groups that have best adjusted to the demands and opportunities of this system tend to be the best politically organized, leading to "political complementarities" that make reform of the system's interlocking components even more difficult.

At least descriptively, Schneider's model fits the Arab world quite well. In the core Arab cases, large firms tend to be similarly diversified and are, if anything, less technologically sophisticated; skills are even less developed; the workforce is even less organized; and levels of cooperation and coordination among firms and between firms and labor are even lower, as formal and informal relationships between market participants remain largely hierarchical (Adly 2020). It is also quite plausible that all these features reinforce each other in a detrimental way. The region differs only with regard to transnational capital, the presence of which in the Arab world is considerably smaller. It remains, by contemporary standards, relatively isolated, with fairly small, often domestically owned manufacturing sectors.

That said, there are critical, mutually reinforcing features that distinguish Arab capitalism which the HME model does not capture. The full set of these is outlined in Figure 1 and empirically illustrated in subsequent sections of the Element. First, a key player structuring Arab capitalism is the state, an actor that Schneider discusses only in passing. The state was not included in the original formulation of VoC, but has been increasingly integrated in more recent contributions (Hancké et al. 2007; Nölke et al. 2015; Schmidt 2009; Schneider 2013; Walter and Zhang 2012). Its deep role as employer, subsidizer, and interventionist regulator in the Arab world is central to the model, adding another level of hierarchy.

Deep intervention by the state is a key cause for the segmentation of both businesses and workers into insiders, who enjoy state support and protection, and outsiders, who do not. Much of Arab business remains dependent on support and protection from the state and vulnerable to state intervention,

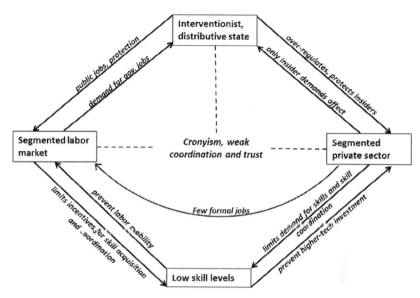

Figure 1 Segmented market economies

even more so than in other regions. The ability to tap state resources and navigate heavy Arab bureaucracies is very unevenly distributed, however. At the top, privileged links to state elites and bureaucracy create a small group of firms with better access to regulation, credit and subsidies, and, as a result, unusually high profits. Most other businesses, particularly smaller firms, remain outsiders whose property rights are uncertain and whose interests are not represented in the policy-making process (Benhassine 2009; Heydemann 2004). These divisions have come to be much better understood in recent years thanks to qualitative case studies and econometric evidence on crony capitalism in the Arab world.

On labor markets, the state also retains a stronger role both as regulator and, crucially, as direct employer. Fairly heavy labor regulations and weak job generation by formal private businesses create a large informal sector, not unlike in other developing countries. But different from most other cases, including in Schneider's Latin America, insiders on the labor market for the most part are formal *public* employees rather than private ones, as formal employment in the weak private sector remains tiny (Gatti et al. 2013). Employment-related ("Bismarckian") social security benefits are unusually generous in the Arab world, yet as they are based on formal work contracts, they increase divisions with outsiders who are excluded from them (Levin et al. 2012). Noncontributory social assistance that would benefit outsiders, while expanding in recent years, remains weak across the region. The divided labor market caters to a relatively large insider group and saps state resources that are diverted from more inclusive and growth-oriented policies.

Segmentation in the Arab world is particularly rigid and hard to overcome in both business and labor market. There is less mobility between segments and barriers to entry are higher – both, again, the result of particularly deep formal and informal state intervention that creates especially pronounced and stable privileges for insiders (Benhassine 2009; Schiffbauer et al. 2015). Despite all "neoliberal" downsizing, Arab capitalism provides more widespread distribution of state resources than in many other developing countries, benefiting a relatively broad middle class. Yet the system remains deeply exclusive for those outside of this coalition.

Rigid insider groups in business and labor market in turn create vested political interests that make economic reforms to reduce segmentation difficult. As we will see, insiders in the Arab world have more to lose than elsewhere, and their insider position is more stable over time, giving particularly strong opportunities and incentives for "opportunity hoarding" (Tilly 1998). As a result, insiders often resist reforms actively, both in authoritarian and democratic systems. Outsiders, for their part, usually demand expansion of insider benefits to them rather than wholesale reform, the benefits of which are less certain and potentially lie only in the distant future. The weakness of the private job market further boosts outsiders' political demands for government jobs (Assaad and Barsoum 2019).

Where and when it exists, interest group politics is centered around better-organized insider interests, not unlike industrial relations in dualistic European labor markets. Encompassing interests that could push for inclusive reforms have weak incentives and opportunities to organize given the complexity of such reforms, their diffuse payoffs, and, in contrast, the immediate threat they can pose to insiders. Political elites are incentivized to privilege insider protection or the occasional expansion of insider privilege to politically salient outsider groups over other policies. This has been most visible in Tunisia, where the region's most powerful union, the Union Générale Tunisienne du Travail (UGTT), mostly represents the large minority of formally employed nationals, leading to periodic tensions with weaker and more dispersed networks trying to rally the majority of unemployed and informally employed.

Like other developing regions, the Arab world is trapped in a low-skills equilibrium in which companies do not invest in technology because the required skills are not available, while students or workers do not invest in skills because they are not in demand (Booth and Snower 1996; World Bank 2008b).

This dynamic is, however, reinforced by segmentation: insider–outsider divisions, ossified privileges, and higher barriers to entry in both labor markets and corporate sectors mean that productive skills are even less needed and rewarded, and hence not acquired. The preference for public employment in particular undermines the formation of skills relevant to the formal private sector (Assaad 2014b; Schiffbauer et al. 2015). Low skills acquisition in turn prevents mobility of labor into better jobs in the limited cases where they are available. Insider–outsider divisions and the organization of vested insider interests also make collective, encompassing coordination on skills or labor standards difficult. The result is low-technology, undiversified production structures.

As in Schneider's model, the key mode of coordination in this type of capitalism is hierarchical, be it between state elites and business or employers and workers – but it is mostly limited to insiders. Different from Latin America, I will demonstrate that there is little mobility between formal and informal status on the labor market, making insider–outsider division a durable organizing principle.

As the following empirical sections will show, even in comparison with other low- to mid-income countries, core Arab economies stand out in a number of characteristics that reflect the aforementioned constellation of forces: despite decades of partial liberalization, state intervention through regulation and subsidization remains comparatively deep. The depth of insider privileges is reflected in unusually large public sector employment and strong wage premia for public sector jobs as well as a striking dominance of large, well-connected private firms. There is unusually low mobility across insider and outsider segments, as reflected, among other things, in the long duration of informality for jobseekers and firms, the rarity of moves between private and public employment, and the small number of formal firms created. Skill levels, firm investment in skills, and returns to skills are all unusually low. I illustrate these patterns with country-level comparative international data in the subsequent sections; they are also summarized with region-level comparisons in the online appendix (Figure O6).

This Element contributes to the broader VoC debate not only by incorporating new cases and developing (yet) another model, but also by outlining more broadly how the interaction of the state with labor markets and firms can be conceptualized in developing country capitalisms. By focusing on insider–outsider dynamics more explicitly, the Element also captures a core dynamic of modern capitalism that political economists to date have mostly discussed with reference to advanced countries (Biegert 2019; Palier and Thelen 2010; Rueda 2007; Thelen 2014). My analysis of segmented labor markets and the political feedback mechanisms maintaining them owes much to comparative political economy literature about labor dualism in Europe – a literature that so far has not been integrated into VoC approaches.

Insider–outsider dynamics on labor markets are even more socially consequential in developing countries with higher levels of inequality, stretched government resources, and unreliable institutions. The full ensemble of these dynamics as documented here for the Arab world is unlikely to be the same in other parts of the Global South – in many passages, this Element does indeed show that it is not. Yet many of the individual mechanisms of segmentation identified here could be usefully investigated in other less developed regions with a view to building up a comparative understanding of labor market and business segmentation in the Global South.

Table 1 provides an overview of how the SEME concept differs from other main VoC models in the literature, including Schneider's. While the SEME concept shares many characteristics of Schneider's HME, the more pronounced role of the state and the centrality and rigidity of insider–outsider segmentation make it a model sui generis with its own feedback mechanisms.

While this Element is critical of accounts that blame the Arab world's ills on marketization, in keeping with the VoC tradition it does not cheerlead neo-liberalism either. Its claim is not that fuller withdrawal of the state from regulation and distribution would have solved the region's economic development issues – the Latin American experience since the 1980s has shown that excessive marketization not only tends to create soaring inequality but, by itself, also does not guarantee high growth (Schneider 2013). In the Arab world, it is not the deep presence of the state per se that hampers economic performance. It is, instead, its very uneven presence. The state's primary function as defender of insiders creates the low dynamism and exclusion that characterize core Arab economies. The resources of Arab states are stretched thin due to its commitments to insider cartels, preventing state-led investment in broader economic development strategies and more inclusive welfare systems.

VoC approaches have been critiqued from many angles. Key arguments include that VoC theories do not allow enough space for change, ignore the state and politics, hew to methodological nationalism, and are ahistorical (see Hancké et al. (2007) for an overview). The SEME concept addresses the critiques directly: first, I show how change often results in a shift of insider–outsider boundaries rather than an end to segmentation, giving SEMEs the ability to accommodate demographic, fiscal, productivity and political crises without abandoning their organizing principles. That said, I comment in the conclusion on how SEMEs could change more fundamentally in the future. Second, like in other more recent VoC formulations (Nölke and Claar 2013; Schmidt 2009; Schneider 2013), the state and political feedback loops are central in my model.

Table 1 Key features of different VoC models

	LME	CME	HME (Schneider)	SEME
Coordination mechanism	Market	Nonmarket, horizontal	Hierarchies	Insider hierarchies
Labor relations	Market-based, shorter-term	Collective bargaining, long-term	Atomized hierarchy, short tenures	Atomized hierarchy, long-term insider protection
Skills formation	Based on market signals	Based on long-term informal, collective cooperation	Undermined by atomized labor relations	Undermined by atomized and exclusive labor relations
Role of state	None	Limited	Complementing hierarchies	Complementing and reproducing hierarchies

Third, while my model is methodologically nationalist, I argue that this approach is more warranted in the Arab world than in most other regions. Economic globalization and the presence of foreign capital are comparatively limited and a key SEME characteristic is precisely that the state protects insiders from these forces. The SEME concept helps to explain the specific ways in which countries adjust to global pressures. Finally, while I cannot establish the full historical origins of the SEME model, the next section shows some of its historical roots in the post-independence era of Arab nationalism, in which transnational ideological competition contributed to entrenching particularly ambitious states across the region.

2 Historical Roots

My SEME argument constitutes a (complex) causal story of interlocking parts and feedback loops. Its main focus, however, is on what keeps the current equilibrium stable, not on the historical causes that established it in the first place. That said, we know that state regulation, distributional structures, and coalitions are deeply path-dependent (Collier and Collier 1991; Pierson 2000). Understanding the current institutional equilibrium in the Arab world, and the relative differences between cases, requires at least a high-level investigation of the region's long history of ambitious state intervention.

There are limits to what can be done in a short monograph. The main focus here is, therefore, on shared factors – especially the diffusion of the Arab nationalist state-building model from the 1950s on – that help to explain the regional clustering of SEME characteristics. Country-specific histories undoubtedly matter in explaining the specific shapes of state intervention and social coalitions, but these are beyond the reach of this Element.[6] I also do not engage with "longue durée" theories that seek to explain Arab economic underperformance and private sector weakness with pre-colonial institutional legacies (Blaydes and Chaney 2013; Kuran 2012; Rubin 2017). My focus is on relatively shorter-term factors characterizing the modern economies of the region. Large bureaucracies, formal labor markets, formal firm sectors, and state-orchestrated skill systems – key components of the SEME concept – are mostly creatures of the twentieth century, and the post-independence period in particular. That said, further research to investigate how longer-term institutional legacies have conditioned the emergence of these modern structures would be a worthwhile undertaking.

---

[6] One important factor that has deepened state intervention, employment, and welfare provision in particular countries has been elite conflict (Eibl 2020; Waldner 1999). Low levels of indigenous private sector development were another factor in North African cases in particular (Eibl 2020; Willis 2012).

When the Maghreb and Mashreq countries in the core of the Arab region achieved independence in the 1950s and 1960s, they were poor, underdeveloped, and had small state apparatuses (Diwan and Akin 2015, 18; Owen and Pamuk 1998). Yet they by and large embarked on a more ambitious path of state building than their peers in other developing regions, resulting in consistently high shares of government spending in GDP (Figure 2).

A key part of the story was intense ideological competition across the region during the era of Arab nationalism in the 1950s and 1960s, a family of ideologies that held genuine mass appeal and proposed state-oriented, populist economic programs (Ayubi 1995; Heydemann 1999; Waterbury 1983).

The region's nationalist republics Algeria, Egypt, Iraq, Syria, and, to a lesser extent, Tunisia and Yemen were the most ardent proponents of such policies (Ayubi 1995; Cammett et al. 2015; Henry and Springborg 2010; Owen and Pamuk 1998). While the programs led to considerable improvements in education and life expectancy, they also brought about deep state involvement in economic life. The Arab republics nationalized strategic sectors and intervened deeply in the remaining, smaller-scale private economy through restrictive licensing rules, price controls, regulation of labor and production processes, and state-directed credit allocation. They used public sectors as tools of mass employment and introduced heavy subsidies for consumer goods and, from the 1970s on, energy. State-led attempts at import-substituting industrialization further deepened the public sector's role in economic life (Cammett et al. 2015; Henry and Springborg 2010; Heydemann 1999; Waterbury 1983).

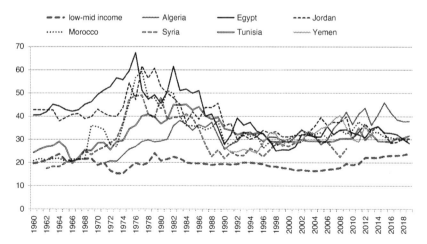

Figure 2 Share of government spending in GDP (percent)
Source: Data courtesy of Ishac Diwan and Tarik Akin (based on International Monetary Fund (IMF) sources).

The following section will provide a more detailed account of the post–World War II economic policies in Egypt, which has served as model for many of its neighbors, and of Syria, which has been the most extreme case of statism among the nationalist Arab regimes of the 1960s and 1970s. The two cases illustrate policy patterns that have been widely copied across the rest of the region, which is discussed more briefly next.

2.1 Egypt and Syria: Pacesetters

Egypt was the first independent Arab country whose conservative monarchy fell to a nationalist revolution in 1952. After a period of relatively moderate economic policy, the nationalization of the Suez Canal in 1956 ushered in a shift toward decidedly etatist economic policy under President Gamal Abdel Nasser. The drive toward socialism peaked in the early 1960s with wide-ranging nationalizations of sectors like banking, heavy industry, and transport, and arrests of leading capitalists. Wide-ranging land reforms set an ownership ceiling to break up large landholdings. Smaller-scale traders and manufacturers escaped from the nationalization drive yet were subject to price controls and other heavy regulations. Foreign trade and currency transactions were tightly state-controlled (Hansen and Nashashibi 1975). In the words of John Waterbury (1983, 77), the leading political economist of post-independence Egypt, "Few developing countries other than those that are professedly Marxist ever cut so deeply into their private sectors as Egypt." Competition for regional ideological leadership in an era of febrile nationalism was one driver for Nasser's increasing radicalism as he "sought to steal the thunder of the [nationalist] Ba'ath Party of Syria and Iraq" (Waterbury 1983, 79).

Deep intervention in the private sector was accompanied by large-scale rent distribution and redistribution policies boosting the consumption power of the Egyptian lower and middle classes. Nasser introduced a 90 percent tax rate for higher earners in 1961, which was increased to 95 percent in 1965 (Waterbury 1983, 75, 77). Also in 1961, his government issued a formal guarantee to employ all university graduates in government, a policy that was extended to secondary school graduates in 1964 (Ayubi 1980, 61; Eibl 2020, 240) and subsequently copied by other Arab states (Bishara 2021). Excess employment by government for the growing educated middle class was a deliberate means of income redistribution in Egypt's "socialist transformation" (Waterbury 1983, 91). At the same time, the state imposed increasingly wide-ranging price controls and extended generous food subsidies (Eibl 2020). Workers and peasants were granted 50 percent representation in Egyptian parliament and other elective bodies.

While these policies boosted consumption, they also came at considerable efficiency costs. The productivity of a civil service that was staffed not in line with functional needs but the supply of jobseekers dropped significantly. Wage growth generally outstripped productivity growth (Ayubi 1980, 244, 251), which became obvious especially in overstaffed and overprotected public enterprises. State-owned Nasr Automotive, for example, produced one-tenth of the cars that rolled out of a Fiat plant in Spain with the same number of workers (Waterbury 1983, 105).

At the end of the 1960s, public consumption as share of GDP reached 25 percent, more than triple its share before the revolution, but savings rates remained as low as in the prerevolutionary 1940s, undermining investment (Hansen and Nashashibi 1975, 15). Nasser's regime clearly privileged consumption, and short term consumer interests, over production (Waterbury 1983, 85, 213). This spending- and consumption-heavy, domestically focused, low accumulation model is the mirror image of the savings- and export-oriented developmental statism that has allowed rapid industrialization in East Asia.[7] It has characterized the Egyptian economy, and most other economies in the region, ever since (Adly 2020).

The "populist authoritarianism" that emerged in Syria in the 1950s and 1960s resembles the Egyptian social and economic model closely but has taken intervention and redistribution even further (Heydemann 1999); it proved especially resilient until Syria's descent into civil war in 2011. Syria was particularly exposed to the ideological competition during the post–World War II heyday of Arab nationalism. Nasser enjoyed unrivaled popular support across the region after the Suez Crisis of 1956 and explicitly sought to export Egypt's social and political model to other Arab countries (Heydemann 1999, 74, 82). Other socialist-leaning, anti-bourgeois variants of Arab nationalism, notably Ba'athism, also quickly spread in Syria. The most dramatic expression of Syria's susceptibility to transnational Arabist ideology was its formal union with Egypt from 1958 to 1961, initiated by Arab nationalists in the Syrian regime who sought to leverage Nasser's popularity to sideline local political rivals (Mufti 1996).

The Egyptian administrators sent to Syria during the union period brought with them many of Nasser's economic policy innovations. The union government imposed a wide range of price, supply and import controls, subjected industrial production and commerce to numerous new licensing requirements, set ceilings on private profits, and introduced state control over foreign exchange. In July 1961, at the same time as in Egypt, Nasser decreed wide-ranging nationalizations (Heydemann 1999, 88, 98, 99, 107, 129).

---

[7] Latin American economies have often been described in these terms (Dornbusch and Edwards 1991), but the pattern is arguably both more extreme and more resilient in core Arab cases.

The United Arab Republic collapsed in September 1961 in the wake of a countercoup in Syria. Yet the basic framework for a deeply interventionist economic regime had been created and was further deepened during the rule of various Ba'ath Party factions from 1963 to 1970 (Heydemann 1999, 163), who in turn engaged in ideological competition with the rival left-leaning Ba'ath regime in Iraq (Kienle 1990). During that period, the government marginalized Syrian landholding elites and undertook large-scale land redistribution, deepened state control of external trade, and nationalized more industries, eventually resulting in public ownership of three-quarters of the national economy (Heydemann 1999, 189, 190). The public sector's share in capital formation peaked at 69 percent in the 1970s (Mufti 1996, 248).

As in Egypt, the state apparatus was used as a job creation machine for a growing state-dependent middle class and soon became the employer of choice for most citizens (Heydemann 1999, 60, 152; Hinnebusch 2004, 130). A deliberate policy of overemployment resulted in dramatic expansion of the public payroll (Heydemann 1999, 175, 177; Waldner 1999, 87), and the government started subsidizing a wide reach of consumer goods to buttress its support in the wider population (Waldner 1999, 74, 87). Workers and peasants were mobilized and controlled through newly centralized, state-controlled unions (Heydemann 1999, 122, 201 f.). By the late 1960s, "norms of distributive justice and popular welfare... had become integrated into Syrian politics" (Heydemann 1999, 175). These expectations should prove very resilient.

As in Egypt, the Syrian government privileged broad-based, state-supported consumption over savings, resulting in low investment rates (Hinnebusch 2004, 127 f.; Waldner 1999, 129 f.). Waldner calls this regime "precocious Keynesianism" – a shift toward mass consumption before the creation of a broad industrial basis that could generate income to maintain this consumption in the long run (1999). While coined for the Syrian case, the concept is applicable across most of the Arab region.

In both Egypt and Syria, the nationalist phase of the 1960s left a deep legacy of bureaucratic control of production processes and a deep legacy of broad-based, middle-class-oriented distribution, particularly through excess state employment.

2.2 Republican Followers in the Region

Other republics in the core Arab world followed a similar template. Tunisia, while known as an early economic liberalizer from the 1970s on, underwent a deep, explicitly socialist phase in the 1960s under President Bourguiba and his powerful minister of planning and finance, Ahmed ben Saleh (Ehteshami and Murphy 1996; Eibl 2020; Willis 2012). The country saw a Nasserist-style program of nationalizations, wage and price controls, protectionist trade policies, as well as quick expansion of generous state employment, subsidies, and other welfare mechanisms (Eibl 2020; Murphy 1999). While elite rivalries and Ben Saleh's close links to the international trade union movement played key roles in Tunisia's drive toward socialism, the "general wave of Arab socialism of that era" also mattered (Murphy 1999, 80). After Ben Saleh was sidelined in 1969 and fled into exile in 1973, he remained active in radical Arab nationalist politics (Jebari 2020).

Next to Syria, Algeria is the core Arab country with the deepest track record of statism. Senior leaders of the National Liberation Front ruling party figures had spent time in Cairo in the 1950s under Nasser's protection. When Algeria became independent of France in 1962, it embarked on a typical Arab socialist path of deep intervention in the economy, protectionism, generous state employment, and subsidy provision, boosted by revenues from oil fields that had been discovered in the 1950s. The regional framing of the regime's ideology declined with the removal of President Ben Bella in 1965, who had been close to Nasser, and yielded to a broader "Third Worldist" orientation. Yet the state intervention in the economy continued to deepen, particularly with the 1970s oil boom which allowed the building of large-scale public industries (Malley 1996; Willis 2012).

Another country that was unusually directly exposed to Egyptian influence was North Yemen: during the country's civil war from 1962 to 1970, the republican-nationalist side, which had removed the old monarchy through a coup, was a client of Nasser's Egypt, which tried to burnish its Arab nationalist credentials through a proxy war against conservative Saudi Arabia. While 60,000 Egyptian soldiers fought on the republican side, thousands of Egyptians bureaucrats and teachers ran the fledgling Northern Yemeni state, in which local Nasserists and other Arab nationalists played key roles (Burrowes 2016, 24; 2005). North Yemen never had the resources to engage in ambitious state-building efforts as the relatively richer and more developed countries of the Maghreb and Mashreq; below a veneer of modern ideologies, its policies have remained shot through with tribal factionalism. Yet it embarked on a broadly similar course of deep state intervention in the economy, protectionism, growing state employment, and provision of energy subsidies (Burrowes 2016, 153; 2010, 356).

The other state in modern Yemen's territory, the People's Democratic Republic of Yemen (1967–90), emerged from an anti-colonial struggle that was led by a coalition of Arab nationalist and Marxist forces, and was the only Arab country to officially declare its adherence to Marxism as ruling ideology. It embarked on a socialist campaign of nationalization and central planning from the late 1960s, although with very limited resources (Lackner 1985). With the collapse of the Soviet Union, the two Yemens agreed to merge in 1990, followed by a brief civil war and reunification under Northern dominance in 1994, retaining a legacy of statism. In sum, all republics in our case have undergone prolonged periods of statist-populist development and state expansion, often emerging from the era of Arab nationalist competition.

2.3 Monarchies under Pressure

The Arab world in the 1950s and 1960s was a densely connected ideological space in which pan-Arab ideas and political subversion flowed freely across borders. Malik Mufti counts a total of seventeen pan-Arab merger and unity projects, a list that involved each of our core cases at some point (Mufti 1996). In this context, the populist distributional policies of the first nationalist republics – which had mostly emerged from nationalist coups against conservative monarchs (Kerr 1965) – put pressure on other regimes in the region to play catch-up in controlling the national economy to provide broader middle-class benefits to their restless populations. This included conservative monarchies that on the face of it seemed to provide an inhospitable environment for statist and redistributive economic policy.

As most post–World War II states and ruling elites across the region were unconsolidated, they remained susceptible to external pressures. For Mufti (1996), this explains their willingness to engage in unification schemes, which helped them to outmanoeuver domestic rivals and improve their popular legitimacy. He argues that regional rivalries led to ambitious state-building efforts across the region (Mufti 1996, 13). I would add – and illustrate in this section – that such pressures specifically explain the rapid spread of the statist and populist economic models associated with Arab nationalism after 1956, which were deployed to counter the ideological pressures and promises of radical nationalist movements. Arab union projects and inter-Arab rivalry were the most intense from 1955 to 1967 (Mufti 1996, 5), which is also the era when the foundations of the region's modern political economies were laid.

This process was particularly visible in Jordan, which was positioned at the fulcrum of regional ideological competition for much of post–World War II Arab history (Peters and Moore 2009; Robins 2004). Already before the Nasserist period, it had engaged in abortive union schemes with Syria (Mufti 1996, 47). As a result of relative free elections in October 1956 – just on the heels of the Suez Crisis – King Hussein was forced to appoint a Nasserist cabinet (Mufti 1996, 79). Prime Minister Suleiman Nabulsi, a committed left-wing Arab nationalist, explained in December 1956 that "Jordan cannot live forever as Jordan" (Dann 1989, 45). Briefly after Nabulsi's forced resignation in April 1957, the country saw a high-level Nasserist coup attempt. Although it was thwarted, Jordan continued to face acute threats from Nasserist and Baathist officers (Mufti 1996, 117, 122). After the Six-Day War of 1967, the Nasserist and Ba'athist threats combined with new pressures from Jordan-based Palestinian guerilla groups who received pan-Arab support (Tell 2013, 126). During a 1975 visit to Amman, President Hafez al-Assad of Syria called Jordan and Syria one country, and the crowds receiving him exclaimed "one people, one army" (Mufti 1996, 239).

The only way for King Hussein to counter nationalist and Arabist demands – and to maintain Jordan as an independent country – was to provide many of the same benefits to Jordanians that his "Arab socialist" rivals provided to their populations. He built up a wide-ranging patronage system that relied heavily on state employment, particularly military jobs with extensive social benefits (Tell 2013, 13, 14). The Jordanian army grew from 24,000 men in April 1956 to 55,000 in 1967, and its patronage employment reached virtually every village by the end of this period (Tell 2013, 120). Such generosity allowed the "consolidation of Hussein's rule in the face of the challenges from Nasser and the PLO" (Tell 2013, 14). What Tariq Tell (2013, 113) calls "military Keynesianism" benefited especially the East Bank population, but also increasingly incorporated Jordanians of Palestinian extraction.

Palestinian guerillas were sidelined during the bloody "Black September" of 1970 and Arab nationalism gradually subsided in the 1970s, yet expectations of state employment proved to be sticky. Increasing aid payments from Gulf monarchies from the 1973 oil shock on in fact boosted Jordanian statism, resulting in an "overdeveloped state apparatus" (Tell 2013, 126, 138). The number of (nonmilitary) civil servants increased from 27,000 in 1970 to 74,000 in 1985 (Jreisat 1989, 99). Government intervention in the economy deepened with the creation of an Egyptian-style "Ministry of Supply" in 1974, increasing price regulations, and the introduction of a range of subsidies to placate consumers (Robins 2004, 152, 153). Jordan kept a relatively liberal trade regime (Wilson 1988). It also did not develop as extensive a public industry as Egypt, Syria, or Algeria – yet its government owned utilities and telecoms, ports, railways, the national airline, cement plants, and the strategically important potash mining sector (Ramachandran 2004). For a formally pro-capitalist monarchy, it leaned rather far toward the Arab statist model.

Morocco, a geo-strategically and culturally more peripheral Arab monarchy with deeper local historical roots, appears to have been under less pressure to follow regional trends, which is consistent with its relatively lesser statist and distributive legacy (Waterbury 1970; Zartman 1987). Its post–World War II rulers have relied more strongly on indirect rule through traditional rural elites, and growth of the Moroccan state has been comparatively restrained. That said, it has been affected by Arab nationalist currents at critical junctures and some of its economic policies have followed the regional template. King Mohammed V, its first post-independence ruler, was close to Nasser and Arab nationalism popular among Moroccans in the 1950s. Mohammed's successor Hassan II was openly pro-Western, yet also faced the persistent threat of a Nasserist-style military takeover in the 1960s and 1970s and put down a leftist rebellion in 1973 (Joffe 1988, 214). As late as 1984, Morocco joined Libya for an abortive union scheme, reacting to a union treaty between Algeria, Tunisia, and Mauritania. From the 1960s on, it pursued a number of statist economic policies (Willis 2012, 231), including an import substitution strategy that led to increasingly higher tariffs and a strict import licensing regime in the 1970s (Ferrali 2012). State ownership expanded across various sectors, with the royal court taking an increasingly visible role in the economy. A phosphate boom during the 1970s allowed the government to introduce a number of food subsidies and to grow state employment, albeit from a low basis (Willis 2012, 234).

By the 1970s, Arab rulers had established an "authoritarian bargain" (Desai et al. 2007) under which their autocratic regimes intervened deeply in the economy, more or less marginalizing the local private sector, and promoted popular consumption through state employment and subsidies. The system had a strong middle-class bias as social insurance was tied to formal (usually state) employment, and apart from food subsidies, none of the countries built a social assistance system that would directly support the large number of poor and the informally employed (Levin et al. 2012; Loewe 2010). Yet its social basis was fairly wide in comparison with most other countries in the Global South.

As illustrated in Sections 2.1–2.3, the regional convergence process toward this model was buttressed by intra-republican ideological outbidding as well as reactive copying of the statist template among monarchies. As a result, statism in the core Arab world ran considerably deeper than in most other regions outside of the Communist sphere.

2.4 Retrenchment since the 1960s

Arab states have had to scale back their ambitions and operations ever since the original statist model faced fiscal crises in the 1970s and 1980s, resulting in partial economic liberalization and a gradual, often conflict-ridden down-scaling of distributional commitments (Cammett et al. 2015; Diwan and Akin 2015). Yet, as shown in Figure 2, state spending has remained consistently above the international average. I will again illustrate the process with the Egyptian and Syrian cases, which will serve as examples for an early liberalizer and an Arab socialist straggler, respectively, followed by summary account of the other core cases and some quantitative data on historical trends in regulation across the region.

Just like Egypt led the region into "Arab socialism," it was also the first country among the core Arab nationalist regimes to start the retrenchment and partial liberalization process. It faced its first economic crisis already in the late 1960s, as production and state revenue did not keep up with the Egyptian model's consumption needs in the wake of the Six-Day War in 1967. But the model had taken deep roots by then and created high popular expectations, resulting in a zigzag course of continued state expansion, occasional fiscal crises, and partial retrenchment measures.

After the Yom Kippur War of 1973, Nasser's successor Anwar el-Sadat faced both a failing public sector and a geopolitical opportunity to pivot toward the United States. He reacted with his famous *infitah* ("opening") policy, which dialed down socialist rhetoric and opened a range of opportunities for the private sector, providing new credit and tax incentives, allowing foreign investors to own up to 50 percent of local companies, and offering them import tariff exemptions (Hinnebusch 1985; McLaughlin 1978).

Yet regulation remained heavy, with private projects being encumbered by currency restrictions and a range of licensing requirements (McLaughlin 1978). Partial liberalization combined with big bureaucracy to produce "unprecedented amounts of high-level corruption" under Sadat (Waterbury 1983, 378), as bureaucrats discovered rent-seeking opportunities and started to invest in sectors close to the ones they administered (Ayubi 1989, 71). The resurgent private sector emerging from the process came to be yet another client of the state rather than an independent social constituency. Its productivity and employment record has been weak (Adly 2020).

While private sector opportunities grew, large-scale distribution policies continued and in many ways deepened. From 1971 to 1976, the public sector workforce grew by 5 percent per year (Waterbury 1983, 112). Efforts at retrenchment were limited to reducing the civil service growth rate rather than reversing it, and law 47 of 1978 gave civil servants further wide-ranging protections (Schmoll 2017). State growth continued into the Mubarak era in the 1980s: in 1986–7, five million Egyptians out of a total labor force of perhaps thirteen million worked for the state and public enterprises (Ayubi 1989, 62), and annual growth of bureaucratic employment continued at 5.6 percent from 1988 to 1998 (Adly 2020, 106). While growth slowed in the 2000s, the state apparatus remained huge, privileging the consumption needs of state-employed insiders. The ruling elite is aware of the legacy of excess employment: in 2019, Egyptian President Abdel-Fattah al-Sisi publicly stated that one million bureaucrats could do the work done by five million (The Economist 2019a). Yet Egyptian rulers have remained constrained by a "moral economy of social entitlements" stemming from the Nasserist era (El-Meehy 2010).

Similar to state employment, the Egyptian subsidy regime continued to expand under Sadat. By the early 1980s, price subsidies required fiscal resources equivalent to more than half of all central governmental expenditures (Waterbury 1983, 213). While subsidies also benefited outsiders in the informal sector, they privileged middle-class recipients given the higher consumption levels of more affluent households. The infamous bread riots of 1977 which followed Sadat's attempt to reduce food subsidies were in fact led by insider clients of the regime such as industrial workers and public sector employees (Eibl 2020, 257; Eibl et al. 2022). Consumer subsidies peaked at 20.5 percent of total expenditures in the 1980–1 budget year (Eibl 2020, 71). They were gradually reduced in subsequent decades yet remained substantially higher than in other world regions (see Section 3.1).

What changed most from the 1970s on is arguably less the scale of distribution than the growing popular claims on state resources. The main factor here was rapid expansion of the education system. Secondary and university education grew at over 20 percent per year between 1969–70 and the early 1980s (Waterbury 1983, 221). This entailed growing expectations of middle-class employment, buttressed not least by the government's formal guarantee of graduate employment that it never formally rescinded under Mubarak, yet increasingly struggled to fulfill (Adly 2020, 101). As a result, a segmentation of outsiders and insiders gradually emerged: public employment, while remaining large in absolute terms, came to be de facto rationed in the face of a growing national labor supply, whereas the government provided limited welfare mechanisms for those outside of the public sector.

Syria followed a similar trajectory to Egypt, yet with much more caution and less space for private capital. When Hafez el-Asad came to power in 1970s, he initiated a "corrective movement" to rein in the more extreme socialist tendencies of the Ba'athist regime and to provide somewhat more space for local investors. The government created tax-free zones for Syrian investors in commerce and industry, removed import quotas, and somewhat reduced state control over trade. Yet it remained less open to FDI and retained a larger state industrial sector. The cautious liberalization phase came to an end in the late 1970s and was partially reversed in the early 1980s. Cooperation with the Soviet bloc and Gulf aid to Syria as frontier state in the conflict with Israel helped finance a broadly unproductive system (Hinnebusch 2004).

A renewed fiscal and foreign exchange crisis in the mid-1980s ushered in another phase of partial reforms under which the government allowed public–private investment in agriculture and reduced state control over trade and basic commodities (Hinnebusch 1997; Joya 2007). Law 10 of 1991 provided new tax breaks and exemptions from tariffs and import restrictions for private investors, including foreign ones who could now in principle engage in any sector of the economy. Their activities continued to be subject to a range of bureaucratic approvals, however, and public industry remained large. In 1990, the state-owned enterprise (SOE) sector still accounted for 73 percent of industrial output (Mufti 1996, 249).

The 2000s saw another wave of partial liberalization, allowing private banks, deregulating the rental sector, creating a local capital market (Seifan 2008), and further liberalizing foreign trade, investment, and other capital flows (Joya 2007). Yet throughout all periods of partial liberalization, state regulations and licensing requirements remained heavy. The new bourgeoisie that emerged from the 1970s on was subordinate to the state (Waldner 1999, 89) and remained so even when private sector opportunities grew in the 1990s (Heydemann 1999, 206 f.). The government added another client group rather than allowing an independent class to develop.

As in Egypt, partial liberalization led to cronyism and the "embourgeoisement" (Hinnebusch 2004, 133) of state elites, but with a particularly large role for the security apparatus, which led to an especially heavy-handed approach toward private investors. The basic pattern has been that the regime's "Alawi barons" take what amounts to protection money from the private sector (Hinnebusch 2004, 135; 1997). Compromised through such coercion, the job creation and diversification impact of private business has been limited (Haddad 2020).

While the regime built up a new private sector constituency, its core distributional commitments to the wider population frayed but were never abandoned. As a share of the total budget, subsidies and other transfer payments increased from 10 percent in 1974 to 21 percent in 1980 (Waldner 1999, 108). The fiscal crisis of the 1980s impacted the real income of public sector employees and brought subsidy reductions, but the core distributional regime remained intact (Heydemann 1999, 208; Waldner 1999, 120). The number of the system's beneficiaries continued to grow: armed forces personnel increased from 257,000 in 1980 to 423,800 in 1990, and civilian government employees from 367,469 to 661,526 (Mufti 1996, 248) – a more than twenty-five-fold increase since the 1950s, when there had been a mere 24,000 civilian employees (Hinnebusch 2004, 191). Anecdotes point to public companies overstaffed by a ratio of ten or more (Hinnebusch 1989, 150). The Syrian welfare regime remained resilient throughout the 1990s (Heydemann 1999, 206) and even Bashar el-Asad's market reforms in the 2000s stopped short of privatizing state-owned companies, downsizing the bureaucracy, or abandoning the consumer subsidy system (Seifan 2008). The share of state employment stayed constant until the breakout of civil conflict in 2011 (Mazur 2021, 71), even if this was insufficient to accommodate all new graduates.

All across the core Arab region, interventionist states had to partially retrench after the 1970s yet retained extensive regulations of private economic activity and distributive commitments to the state-employed middle class, even if it became progressively harder for new entrants to join this class. All countries underwent partial trade liberalization, provided new investment incentives and opened new sectors to private firms, loosened price and currency controls, allowed private credit to flow, and trimmed subsidies. In the majority of cases, the SOE sector was downsized and sometimes partially privatized, while in some cases the land reforms of the 1950s and 1960s were reversed (Eibl 2020; King 2009; Robins 2004; Willis 2012).

Yet while the private sector grew across the region, it remained in the shadow of a state which continued to heavily regulate, protect, and subsidize key sectors. Especially in the formerly socialist republics, deep historical distrust of the bourgeoisie let regimes prioritize control over open competition (Waterbury 1983, 180). This constellation led to unequal access to the state's decision-making and resources, often articulated through overlapping crony networks between state and business (Diwan et al. 2019; Eibl 2020; Robins 2004; Willis 2012, 234, 237; Werenfels 2002). These could take many guises: the Jordanian state would procure subsidized goods via favorite local merchants (Robins 2004, 153); "Moroccanization" policies would allow well-connected local clients to replace foreign investors in 1970s Morocco (Willis 2012, 234); Algerian trade liberalization would move monopolies from SOEs to private regime clients (Willis 2012, 257); relatives of Presidents Zine El Abedine Ben Ali in Tunisia and Ali Abdullah Saleh in Yemen would directly corner lucratice protected sectors (Hill et al. 2013; Nucifora et al. 2014).

The account of how the state penetrated private economic activity has so far been qualitative. We do not have many systematic quantitative measures of the long-term regulatory presence of the state that could put the region in comparative perspective. The only indicator going back far enough for our purposes is the Fraser Institute's "regulation index," which is informed by a libertarian economic philosophy and does little to distinguish appropriate from excessive regulation. While this might create biases, it is worth noting that with the exception of Jordan, state intervention according to the index has remained persistently deeper in our cases than the global average (Figure 3) as well as the

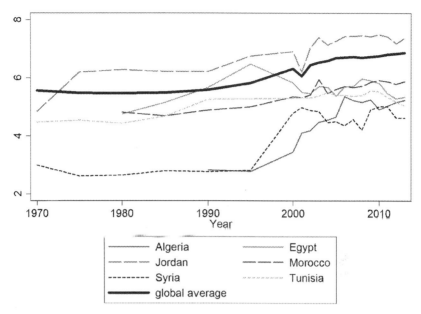

Figure 3 Arab scores on the Fraser "regulation index"
Note: Higher scores indicate lighter regulation.
Source: Fraser Institute.

average of all other world regions (see online appendix, Figure O1). I provide more data in subsequent sections from other, potentially less partial sources to show that regulatory intervention remains deep across the region and that alternative rankings of our cases broadly align with those in the Fraser index. Given that Fraser's potential biases are unlikely to fluctuate strongly over time, this gives us some confidence in its historical data.

Just like deep penetration of the private economy, the distributive role of core Arab states remained sticky throughout decades of partial liberalization. We have already seen that the ratio of state spending to GDP, while falling over time, remained above that of other regions. While public enterprises were downsized and in some cases privatized (Amico and Hertog 2013; El-Haddad 2020a; Willis 2012, 258), regimes continued to expand the core government payroll, even if the share of civil servants shrank in relative terms due to population growth. This contrasts with regions like sub-Saharan Africa, where public employment in several cases more than halved as a result of structural adjustment programs (Simson 2019). Similarly, subsidies, while trimmed in all cases, were never abandoned in the core Arab world. Protests against subsidy reforms succeeded surprisingly often, and even in economically most liberal Morocco, subsidization of food and energy remained the most important component of the social safety net into the 2010s (Eibl 2020, 80). The view that the state was responsible for the provision of basic needs remained widespread (El-Meehy 2010; Schmoll 2017; Willis 2012, 239), even if governments struggled to live up to their historical commitments.

The main change to the political economy of distribution in the region instead was the size of the population making claims on the state, resulting notably from rapid growth in university enrolment since the 1970s. The quality of university programs typically was weak – not least because quantity was prioritized over quality – yet this expansion created much larger strata of labor market entrants with middle-class aspirations (World Bank 2008b; see also Figures 16 and 17 and Section 3.4 on skills). Different from many Latin American and sub-Saharan African countries, no government sector in the region saw large-scale redundancies, highlighting the stickiness of existing distributive entitlements. Yet new entrants have increasingly been excluded from public employment as governments lacked the resources to create even more public jobs. Because the formal private sector has failed to generate significant employment, informal employment has grown among new entrants (Eibl 2020, 242), creating an increasingly visible segmentation between older insiders and younger outsiders on the labor market.

2.5 Summary

Our case narratives as well as available fiscal and regulatory data suggest that fiscal crises and structural adjustment have affected the Arab region like other parts of the developing world – yet relatively speaking, it has retained its distinctly statist profile. As we will see later in the Element, the region's statist legacy remains visible in unusually high levels of public sector employment and bureaucratic penetration of labor markets and businesses activities, reflecting the stickiness of historically established institutions and suggesting that we are observing a resilient equilibrium.

The relative scarcity of state resources and the discretionary nature of state intervention have, however, produced deep divisions between privileged insiders and outsiders in these spheres. While the statist histories of Arab regimes and their economies are relatively well documented, this Element probes their less well-understood divisive consequences in the present day, exploring the equilibria that keep divisions in place and retard more inclusive development for workers and firms.

The following core sections outline the roles of state, business, labor, and skills markets that have emerged from the region's statist history in more detail, elaborating in particular how institutions across these spheres continue to complement and reinforce each other. It will present data on all core Arab countries as available and provide international comparisons where possible. We will see that the core populist republics (Algeria, Egypt, and pre-2010 Syria) are consistently in line with the ideal type (outlined in Figure 1) on practically all measures, while the other core cases fit it more often than not. For a more aggregate view, the online appendix (O6) contains comparisons of the core Arab average with other world regions as well as noncore Middle Eastern cases, again showing how the region stands out.

3 Segmented Market Economies

The Arab state retains a deep presence in the economy through both extensive distribution and deep bureaucratic penetration of markets. Grasping the scale of both is critical for understanding the structure of Arab labor markets, corporate sectors and skills systems, and the ways these interventions benefit insiders.

3.1 Overambitious States

Arab states' distributive and welfare ambitions remain strong. These have produced faster post–World War II increases in schooling years and life expectancy than in any other developing region (Diwan and Akin 2015). A more problematic distributive legacy is their ongoing commitment to large-scale public employment. The share of public employment has been gradually declining in recent decades – yet it remains high in international comparison, with only Morocco lying below the global trend line in Figure 4.[8]

The shares of public employment mostly lie between 20 and 40 percent, far above those in richer Latin America, where they range from 4 to 15 percent (OECD 2014, 61), sub-Saharan Africa, where they range from 2 to 9 percent (Monga and Lin 2015, 138; Simson 2019), and East Asia and Pacific, where they mostly lie below 5 percent (Packard and Van Nguyen 2014, 16).

While public salaries are by no means high, in the cases where we have data, they typically remain higher than in the private sector, especially compared to the informal sector (Assaad 2014b; Gatti et al. 2014, 255; Hertog 2021).

At the same time, despite some liberalization steps, Arab government extensively regulates formal private labor markets, providing fairly high protection for the minority able to land a formal job there. Labor regulations that restrict

---

[8] The Moroccan civil service pays unusually well in international comparison, resulting in a high share of salaries in total state spending despite a relatively small state. Total salary expenditure in 2019 was 11.4 percent of GDP, compared to an average of 6 percent for emerging economies (International Monetary Fund 2021a, 28; Tamirisa and Duenwald 2018, 8).

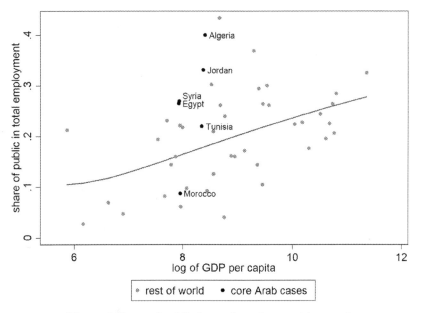

Figure 4 Share of public in total employment (percent)
Source: ILO, national sources.

hiring and firing, while not exceptional, are relatively intense, particularly in the region's republics, and formal benefits are particularly generous (Gatti et al. 2013; Islam et al. 2022). The consequences for the private labor market will be further discussed in Section 3.2.

Arab governments also distribute goods to private business. Key channels are energy subsidies which go to both households and industry and which mostly lie above international averages (Figure 5). As we will see in Section 3.3, these have been a critical currency for crony networks in energy-intensive sectors.

Similarly, the state remains deeply involved in the allocation of land as well as credit, as Arab countries by and large retain higher state ownership in banks than is the case in other regions (Adly 2020; Benhassine 2009, 119; Farazi et al. 2011).

Governments have become increasingly cash-strapped and have cut industrial subsidies during the fiscal crises of recent years. They might well disappear in the coming years. Regulatory intervention and protection remain at least as important for Arab business, however, and have proven stickier.

Some of the heavier regulations of the 1960s statist period have been rescinded or reduced: there are fewer currency and price controls while FDI restrictions have been relaxed. Many remain, however: licensing and inspection regimes, bankruptcy procedures, and labor rules are seen as particularly onerous in the Arab world. Only Tunisia and Morocco rank in the top half of countries in

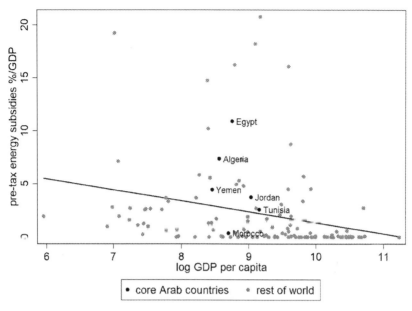

Figure 5 Pre-tax energy subsidies (% of GDP, 2013)
Source: IMF.

the International Finance Corporation's "Doing Business" comparison of country business environments (Figure 6). Similarly, all countries bar Jordan score lower than the international trend line for the Fraser Institute's "regulation index," which attempts to measure the heaviness of regulation across credit markets, labor markets, and business regulations (Figure 7).

Finally, Arab states also remain heavily involved in regulating cross-border trade. All known core Arab cases bar Yemen show an above-average score on the Overall Trade Restrictiveness Index, a compound measure of tariff and nontariff barriers (Figure 8). The data in Figure 8 are somewhat old and Arab countries in North Africa in particular have since reduced tariffs in the context of multilateral trade deals. Yet these have often been replaced by more expansive nontrade protection measures (Ruckteschler et al. 2019). More recent data comparing nontariff measures include only a smaller subset of Arab countries (Egypt, Morocco, and Tunisia), but show continued above-average protection rates (Niu et al. 2018).

Due to the substantial share of state spending in GDP, states remain key drivers of economic demand in the region. There is limited privately driven consumer demand because such a large share of better-paid employment is public and outsiders are relatively poor. The weakness of noncommodity exports further deepens firms' dependency on state spending. Arab states continue to run a state-dependent

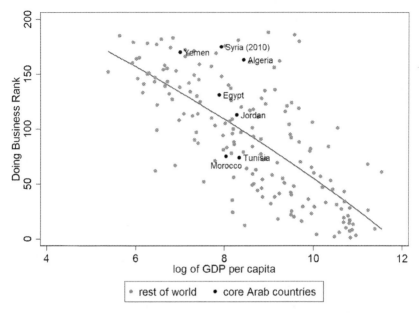

Figure 6 Global "Doing Business" rankings

Note: Smaller means better rank.

Source: IFC.

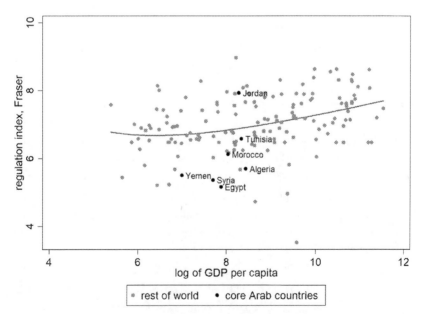

Figure 7 Fraser Institute "regulation index" scores

Note: Higher values imply less regulatory intervention.

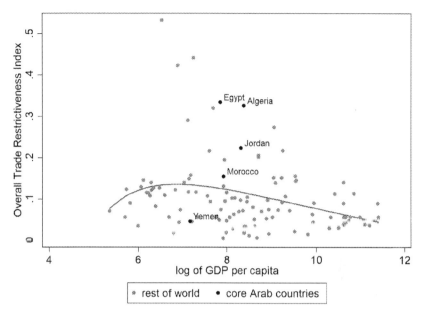

Figure 8 Overall Trade Restrictiveness Index
Source: Kee et al. (2009).

Keynesian growth model, but with weak productive structures and a weak revenue basis (Waldner 1999). The need to stimulate economies and support insiders through public consumption has led to high public debt levels and limited investment: all our cases bar (oil-dependent) Algeria have been operating on higher debt levels than the average country in their income groups, and all but Algeria and Morocco have recorded lower gross fixed capital formation.[9]

3.2 A Segmented Labor Market

State intervention deeply shapes economic incentives and outcomes. In particular, a deep history of state involvement in Arab labor markets has created rigid insider–outsider divisions that in turn are reinforced by political feedback loops.

Arab labor markets are divided into formal public employment, formal private employment, and informal private jobs. The informal labor force – defined as workers not contributing to social security – averages 65 percent across the Arab

---

[9] Average debt/GDP from 2000 to 2017 ranges from 52 to 85 percent for all countries bar oil-rich Algeria (which recorded 24 percent), while the emerging and developing market average was 43 percent. GFCF clustered in the 17–24 percent range, with only Algeria and Morocco reaching 38 percent and 32 percent, respectively, compared to the lower-middle income average of 28 percent. Data from World Development Indicators.

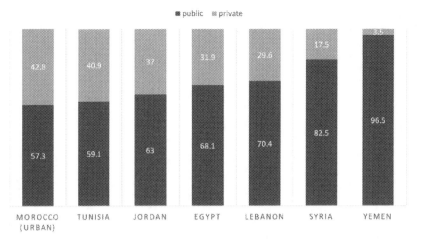

Figure 9 Distribution of formal employment by sector (percent)
Sources: Gatti et al. (2013, 148) and Gatti et al. (2014, 90).

world outside of the Gulf monarchies according to estimates by the International Labor Organization (Intini 2021). This is high, but not higher than in other developing countries (Gatti et al. 2014, 52). What is unusual, however, is the very high ratio within the formal sector of public to private employment (Figure 9), reflecting the region's large and in some cases legendary bureaucracies.

The preponderance of government jobs in the formal sector contrasts with both sub-Saharan Africa and Latin America, where formal private employment is significantly larger than government employment (Galli and Kucera 2004, 815; Monga and Lin 2015, 138). What is more, in line with global trends of labor market dualization even formal private employment in Arab countries has started to be temporary and precarious for new entrants, following rounds of partial labor market liberalization (Assaad 2014a; Assaad et al. 2021). At the same time, due to growing fiscal pressures, rates of government hiring have dropped strongly since the 1980s (Assaad and Barsoum 2019), making it much harder for new labor market entrants to acquire insider status. Fiscal retrenchment has generated deepening segmentation between a large, typically older constituency with public jobs and those without.

3.2.1 Low Mobility across Segments

As important and different from the Latin American cases that Schneider describes, there is little mobility between labor market segments. Very few workers leave the public sector with its security and benefits for private employment (Angel-Urdinola et al. 2015, 11; Gatti et al. 2013, 52). Morocco's 2013 labor force survey indicates that among 870,000 unemployed, more than 500,000 have previously worked in the private sector (most of them probably informally), while only 12,000, or less than 1.4 percent of the total, have previously worked in government. This reflects very high security of tenure in the public sector (Haut Commissariat au Plan, Moroc 2013, 351) – the proverbial immovable bureaucrat often caricatured in Arab popular culture.

In Latin America, by contrast, patronage employment in the public sector typically is subject to considerable political turnover (Schuster 2015). Although evidence is scattered, case literature from various sub-Saharan African countries also documents fairly high public sector turnovers there (Briggs 2007; Musingafi et al. 2013; Pieterson 2014).

In Arab countries, informality moreover typically lasts longer than in other regions before individuals move into another labor market status (Gatti et al. 2013, 153; Gatti et al. 2014, 187). Similarly, long-term unemployment accounts for a disproportionate share of all unemployment (Figure 10), reflecting durable exclusion particularly in the republican cases in Algeria and Egypt. Labor turnover is generally low (Angel-Urdinola, Nucifora, and Robalino 2015, 85; Gatti et al. 2013, 150 f.). In Tunisia, annual layoffs in the private sector are less than 1 percent of the workforce, compared to more than 10 percent in the average OECD country (Angel-Urdinola et al. 2015, 84).

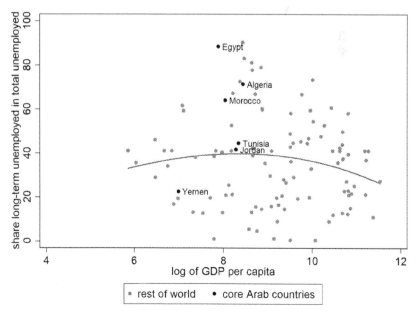

Figure 10 Share of long-term unemployed among all unemployed (percent)
Source: World Bank Development Indicators.

All this indicates that the insider–outsider system in the region's labor market, although generous to a fairly large share of the population, is particularly rigid and inflexible: outsiders stay outsiders for longer and insiders very rarely lose their insider status. Street vendors like Mohamed Bouazizi remain stuck in place, while bureaucrats in Egypt's Mugamma remain safe.

This is confirmed by existing econometric research on labor market transition matrices which measure the incidence of transfers between different labor market states, including inactive, unemployed, formal private, formal public, and informal employment. While time periods and definitions of sectors vary across sources, transfer rates are systematically lower for Arab countries on which we have data – Algeria, Egypt, and Jordan – than for sub-Saharan African and Latin American countries as well as Turkey (see Table 2). There are no sector-specific transition rate estimates for Tunisia, but Yassine (2015) shows that Tunisians generally remain in the same job even longer than Egyptians and Jordanians, reflecting particularly low mobility.

Calculation methods, sample sizes, and definitions of sectors can differ, so the above is only indicative. Yet at least one paper (Woldemichael et al. 2019) provides a direct comparison of Egypt with a number of sub-Saharan African countries. It has a considerably lower standardized "mobility index" score compared to South Africa and Ethiopia (the score for Nigeria is similar, but data for this case are very limited).

Public sector employment used to be a conduit of social mobility and relative egalitarianism in the Arab world, especially for jobseekers from less privileged backgrounds – including for past political leaders from lower-income families like Egypt's Nasser, Syria's Assad, or Tunisia's Ben Ali, who climbed the ranks of their countries' expanding military apparatus before coming to political prominence. But the rationing of state jobs for new entrants has now become a driver of social exclusion (Assaad et al. 2021). Given the weakness of the formal private sector, new labor market entrants are more likely than ever to remain stuck in informal jobs, especially if they come from lower class backgrounds (Alazzawi and Hlasny 2016; Assaad et al. 2021). Across the region, 86 percent of workers in the fifteen to twenty-four age bracket are in informal jobs, compared to 64 percent of the total (Intini 2021).

Figure 11 shows how labor markets in four core Arab countries have come to be segmented by age, with older generations typically enjoying better access to formal government jobs (up to early pensions ages in the fifties), while formal private sector jobs are either negligible in number or also concentrated among older workers. The pattern is similar for both female and male labor force participants, although women, whose general labor force participation rates in

Table 2 Estimated annual transition rates out of formal work[10]

	% Individuals Leaving Formal Employment	% Individuals Leaving Public Sector	% Individuals Leaving Private Sector	Source
Algeria	>4.4%			Adair and Bellache 2014
Egypt	>3.8%	>3.5%	>9.7%	Tansel and Ozdemir 2014
	>1.0%			Wahba 2009
	>6.5%			Woldemichael et al. 2019
Jordan	>2.5%	>2.9%	>3.9%	Gatti et al. 2013
Turkey	10.7%			Tansel and Kan 2012
Argentina	>10%			Bosch and Maloney 2010[11]
Brazil	9.0%			Filho 2012
	>10%			Bosch and Maloney 2010
Mexico	17.6%			Maloney 1999
	>10%			Bosch and Maloney 2010
Ethiopia	>10.1%			Woldemichael et al. 2019
Ghana	32.4%	31.40%	32.60%	Falco and Teal 2012
South Africa	>7.3%			Woldemichael et al. 2019
	>6.5%			Cassim et al. 2016
Uganda	>10.4%	>8.9%	>13%	Kavuma et al. 2015

[10] Most transition matrices in the literature contain the probabilities of transition over periods longer than one year. We divide the transition rates by the period length in years to obtain a rough figure for the annual transition rate. These are lower boundary estimates because individuals can transition more than once over several years (which would count as individual transition every time in annual statistics, but only once in multi-year statistics).

[11] Bosch and Maloney (2010) only show the mean duration of formal employment, which is around five years for all three cases. Assuming that duration of employment, like most zero-bound duration variables, is right-skewed, we can assume that median duration is shorter, so that more than 50 percent of employees leave their formal job within five years, leading to a minimal annual transition rate of 10 percent.

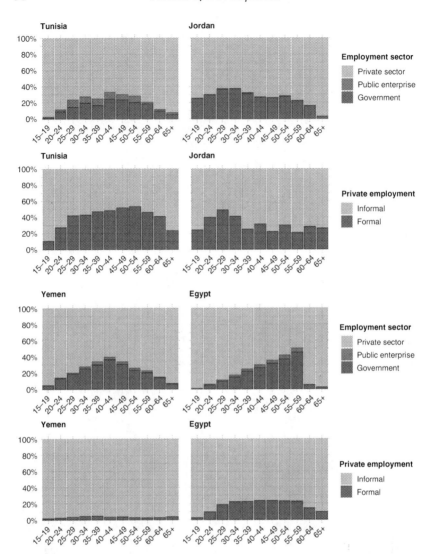

Figure 11 Age distribution of employment by sector and formality

Sources: Surveys obtained from Economic Research Forum (ERF). http://erf.org.eg/data-portal/ –

Egypt – Labor Force Survey 2018; OAMDI, 2021. Harmonized Labor Force Surveys (HLFS). Version 1.0 of Licensed Data Files; LFS 2018 – Central Agency for Public Mobilization and Statistics (CAPMAS).

Tunisia – Labor Market Panel Survey 2014; OAMDI, 2016. Labor Market Panel Surveys (LMPS). Version 2.0 of Licensed Data Files; TLMPS 2014.

Jordan – Labor Market Panel Survey 2016; OAMDI, 2018. Labor Market Panel Surveys (LMPS). Version 1.1 of Licensed Data Files; JLMPS 2016.

Yemen – Labor Force Survey 2013–2014; OAMDI, 2017. Harmonized Labor Force Surveys (HLFS). Version 1.0 of Licensed Data Files; LFS 2013–2014 – ILO and Central Statistical Organization (CSO), Yemen.

the region are unusually low, tend to have a somewhat higher proportion (if a lower absolute number) of formal employees.

The generational dividing lines run within many families, where children are often more educated but parents enjoy much better income. While this can create awkward family dynamics, it also means that younger labor market entrants can often rely on parental support and afford to queue at least for a while (if often in vain) for government jobs.

The one exception to the pattern of generational segmentation is Jordan, which, thanks to its relatively larger fiscal resources (derived largely from geopolitical rents), managed to offer a fairly high share of government positions to younger jobseekers after the Arab uprisings – although at the cost of an unsustainable government debt load that reached 90 percent of GDP in 2021.

3.2.2 Drivers of Segmentation

There are several drivers for the deeper segmentation of Arab labor markets. Apart from the relatively tight regulation of formal private employment that disincentivizes hiring and firing, these include the prevalence of rigid and exclusive informal networks on labor markets, the relative generosity and rigidity of public sector employment, and contribution-based social security systems that are hard to get into and which privilege insiders (another key factor, the segmented private sector's weak ability to create formal jobs, is discussed in Section 3.3).

Rigid and Nepotistic Private Labor Markets

As in other regions, the segmentation of the private labor market into formal and informal is to some extent caused by state regulation of the formal sector. While hiring and firing restrictions have been relaxed substantially over the years (Cammett and Posusney 2010; Hartshorn 2019), redundancies remain fairly difficult. Similar to some European labor markets with high levels of job security for permanent staff (Palier and Thelen 2010), employers are reluctant to hire on open-ended contracts because workers can be hard to dismiss. The costs of employment-based rather than tax-financed social security further disincentivizes the creation of permanent formal jobs (Assaad et al. 2021; Gatti et al. 2013).

Arguably more specific to the region, insider–outsider divisions are bolstered by ineffective human resource management and nepotism in Arab private companies, which are themselves weak and divided into insiders and outsiders (see Section 3.3). Unusually high shares of jobseekers find their positions through friends or relatives (Gatti et al. 2014, 187). Both qualitative and quantitative researchers report that informal social connections are playing a growing role in economy and society (Binzel 2011; El-Said and Harrigan 2009). Formal private

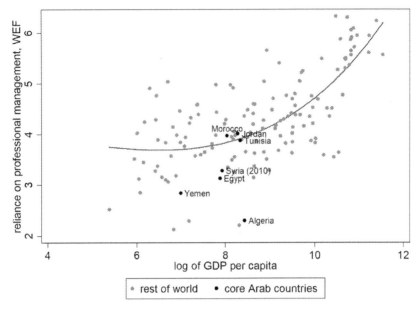

Figure 12 Reliance on professional management (WEF)
Note: Higher score implies more reliance on professional management.
Source: WEF executive opinion survey.

sector jobs in Egypt and Tunisia are largely restricted to educated individuals of privileged socioeconomic background, suggesting an important role for social networks (Assaad et al. 2021).

Confirming a picture of network-driven hiring, the World Economic Forum (WEF) finds that in the majority of Arab countries, including all republics, senior management positions are unusually often held by friends and relatives rather than by professionals chosen by merit (Figure 12). Young Arabs frequently decry the pervasiveness of "wasta," or reliance on informal connections for getting ahead in life. Our data suggest that this phenomenon is not just anecdotal.

Gatti et al. (2013, 167) describe a "meritocracy deficit" that in turn reduces incentives among youth to seek the education and skills relevant for private jobs. Low skills in the population in return abet nepotism, which is further buttressed by limited competitive pressures on Arab firms (Gatti et al. 2014, 160; see also Section 3.3).

Segmentation through State Employment

State employment has an obvious direct impact on labor market segmentation: it nowadays is available only for a (relatively) privileged minority and, once obtained, incumbents practically never give it up. Public employment across the region is not only large, but also on average better paid than private employment (the opposite is the case in Latin America; Inter-American Development Bank, 2004, 171). This claim might not be intuitive after years of inflation-driven real income losses for many Arab civil servants, much decried in both academic literature (Beissinger et al. 2015; Kandil 2012) and popular discourse. Yet regression analysis of labor force survey data from four core Arab countries shows that hourly pay continues to be considerably better for government employees, especially if compared to the large majority of informally employed in the private sector.

Controlling for a range of socioeconomic factors, being employed in the formal private sector rather than government is correlated with an estimated reduction of hourly pay between .12 and .19 on the log scale, corresponding to an 11–17 percent drop. The penalty for being informally employed in the private sector is generally worse – with the exception of Jordan, where estimates are very imprecise – and range all the way to .4 on the log scale, corresponding to a 33 percent reduction (Figure 13; I use the presence of social security as a proxy for formality in the cases of Egypt and Yemen).[12] Most government jobs in the region are by no means a great proposition, yet Arab workers in the private sector are, on average, considerably worse off.

Apart from hourly pay, public sector fringe benefits also tend to be better and working days shorter (Gatti et al. 2013, 150; Haut Commissariat au Plan, Moroc 2013, 272). Paid leave and social security tend to be more generous, job security is higher, holidays are longer, and many civil servants enjoy attractive early retirement options (Assaad and Barsoum 2019; Barsoum and Abdalla 2020). Many Arab public servants resort to informal work on the side to top up their modest salaries – yet they do so on top of a guaranteed source of income and social security that is not available to those in full-time informal employment. After years of fiscal crisis and retrenchment, insiders might be worse off relative to their own past status, but they still enjoy considerable relative privilege.

Perhaps less obviously, Arab state employment practices also indirectly impact the fluidity and efficiency of the private labor market as it impacts new labor market entrants' jobseeking strategies. Government employment remains more attractive for the typical, nonelite jobseeker. As a 2010 Gallup poll shows, the desire for government employment remains high across most of the region,

---

[12] The coefficient plots are derived from regressions that take logged hourly wages as dependent variable and which control for age, age squared, urban versus rural residence, gender, occupation and, where available, region/governorate, marital status, and union membership. Survey weights were applied in all cases but Yemen, where the original data contain no weight variable.

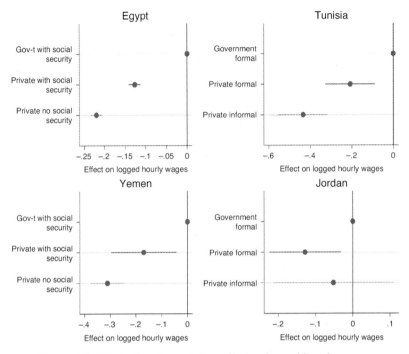

Figure 13 Effect of sector and formality on logged hourly wages
Sources: See Figure 11

especially among graduates (Figure 14). The reasons for this are unlikely to be cultural but lie in the incentives created by the much better work conditions in the public sector.

On average, only about a fifth of respondents preferred private employment (with the remaining respondents voicing no preference). More recent data from the Arab Youth Survey indicate essentially the same pattern (Asda'a BCW 2019, 21). 2014 labor survey data from Tunisia show that 67 percent of Tunisian labor market participants would prefer a government job over a similar private sector job at the same wage; only 19 percent would choose the private job – and even an otherwise similar private job with 50 percent higher wages is only preferred by 28 percent.[13] Similarly, official 2018 labor survey data show that government remains the employer of choice for 83 percent of unemployed Egyptians (Barsoum and Abdalla 2020).

---

[13] Tunisia – Labor Market Panel Survey 2014; OAMDI, 2016. Labor Market Panel Surveys (LMPS), http://erf.org.eg/data-portal/. Version 2.0 of Licensed Data Files; TLMPS 2014. Egypt: Economic Research Forum (ERF).

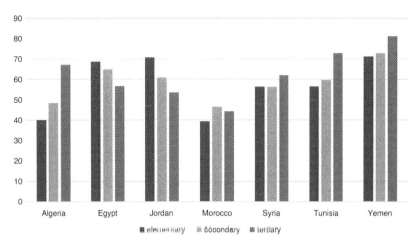

Figure 14 Share of respondents preferring a government job, by education level
(percent)
Source: Gallup polls (2010) (analysis provided by Ishac Diwan).

In his analysis of Mexican data, Maloney (2004) has found limited evidence that privately employed informal workers would prefer a formal job and documents high mobility between informal and formal employment. The Arab world evinces the opposite pattern: formal, particularly government employment is coveted but mobility between different forms of employment is low.

Generous public sector employment not only provides rigid insider privilege. Expectations of public employment increase general reservation wages across the economy (Assaad 2014b; Gatti et al. 2013, 22). They also lead to unproductive and stagnant "queuing" behavior during which jobseekers remain idle until a government job becomes available (Gatti et al. 2014, 256; Gatti et al. 2013, 147; World Bank 2008a, 48 f.), a strategy that is open mostly to young Arabs from better-off families – itself a mechanism that makes it more likely that insider and outsider status are inherited across generations.

As a result, the school-to-work transition in the region is substantially longer than anywhere else (Manacorda et al. 2017). Case evidence from Jordan and Syria, moreover, shows that jobseekers actively avoid private job searches so as to be able to remain eligible for government jobs (Gatti et al. 2014, 256; World Bank 2008a, 48 f.).

Public employment also distorts incentives for skills acquisition – not only because the formal education required for government jobs is often irrelevant for private employment but also because government recruitment, just like

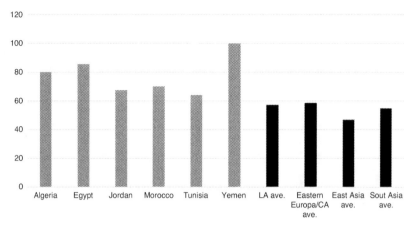

Figure 15 Gross replacement rates, by level of earnings and region (percentage of individual earnings)
Source: Based on Whitehouse (2007).

private recruitment, is widely perceived as nepotistic, hence not meriting particular effort to acquire skills (Brixi et al. 2015; El-Gammal 2013; Gatti et al. 2013, 190).

Excessive Insider Welfare

Governments further deepen labor market segmentation through welfare policies built around generous social security mechanisms that are historically associated with formal employment. Due to the prevalence of informality, less than one-third of the workers in the Arab region contribute to formal social security (Intini 2021). Pensions cover only about a third of the regional population (Robalino 2005). This is not unusual per se in international comparison: the overall Arab average is similar to that in Latin America, yet lies above those in South Asia and sub-Saharan Africa (Gatti et al. 2013, 23), reflecting a relatively large insider coalition in the Arab world.

Where the Arab region stands out is the particularly steep difference between insider privileges and what is available for outsiders. This is reflected in the unusual generosity of most formal pension schemes, which different from other regions often still operate on a defined benefit basis. In many cases these allow or even encourage early retirement and in some instances offer replacement rates above 100 percent, that is, provide benefits that exceed pre-pension income (Figure 15). This is far above what is available in other regions: replacement rates in known cases in sub-Saharan Africa and Asia cluster around 40 percent (Stewart and Yermo 2009; OECD 2013).

As a result, despite the relative youth of Arab populations, Arab pension systems are incurring unsustainable deficits, potentially crowding out other, more inclusive forms of social spending (Jawad 2015) and by and large benefiting an older generation of formal Arab workers. Given the region's low general income levels, these arrangements do by no means provide for a particularly comfortable life – yet given the general scarcity of resources, the relative privilege for insiders is striking.

Even in comparison with other developing countries, Arab states stand out in the limited provision and lopsided nature of noncontributory social safety net programs such as cash benefits, microcredit, workfare, and training initiatives that could benefit those outside of formal employment. Such programs only amount to an average of 1 percent of GDP across the Arab world (World Bank 2018, 19–20), are deeply fragmented, and have coverage rates far below those in other developing regions (Angel-Urdinola et al. 2015, 7, 118; Levin et al. 2012, xxiv). There is variation across the region: Egyptian social assistance is particularly meager, while Tunisia and Morocco provide more; postrevolutionary Tunisia in particular has seen some expansion of social safety and a lively discussion around universal protection. Yet the MENA region as a whole has the lowest mean ratio of social safety spending to GDP of all world regions bar South Asia, and the ratio for all core Arab countries apart from Morocco lies below that regional mean (Morocco barely exceeds the mean; World Bank, 2018, 19–20). Even where social safety is relatively more generous, its scale and scope pales relative to insiders' welfare privileges.

Outside of Palestine, most social assistance program have had little effect on poverty rates, indicating that they often in practice benefit insiders (Ghaith and Abu Shama 2015; Jawad 2015). Governments have experimented with new social assistance mechanisms in the course of partial subsidy reforms in recent years, but more timidly than in most other regions, and coverage of the poor remains bad (ESCWA 2016, 2020, 49; Jawad 2015; Osorio and Soares 2017). Informal workers such as cleaners, garbage collectors, or street vendors typically work the longest hours, in the most precarious jobs, yet also receive by far the least support.

Universal social safety policies could in principle lessen the segmentation of labor markets into formal and informal through unemployment assistance, cash benefits, microcredit programs, and active labor market policies, all of which can facilitate skill acquisition and ease the transition into formal employment – but Arab governments by and large have limited resources or capacity for these. They instead prioritize insiders.

Our findings on stark insider–outsider divisions align with Nita Rudra's work on welfare states in the developing world: she classifies all core Arab cases included in her research as "protective welfare states" that shield select individuals from the market rather than providing general market-oriented welfare like many other countries in the Global South do (Rudra 2007). Under conditions of modern capitalism, such protection from the market can almost by definition only apply to a subset of individuals.

To sum up, Arab governments are deeply involved in providing labor protection, jobs, and social security, but do so in a costly and exclusive way that creates rigid insider–outsider divisions. These are reinforced by unmeritocratic recruitment practices among badly managed but sheltered private businesses. While formal workers, especially in the public sector, are well-protected (and hence cling to their jobs), the state does little for labor market outsiders. The region's main de facto and de jure welfare mechanisms are exclusive state employment and contribution-based social security, respectively, while there is little welfare coverage for informal employees. Informal workers are often an afterthought in systems that have come to cater to a shrinking and economically stagnant yet privileged middle-class constituency under direct protection of the state – a constituency that in turn has little interest in encompassing social safety provision.

While this setup is unusual by standards of low- to mid-income countries, it is not globally unique: continental European labor markets, in Southern Europe in particular, are also divided into well-protected insiders with extensive benefits (albeit more frequently employed in the private sector) and precarious outsiders with minimal welfare (Dolado 2016; Palier and Thelen 2010). Survey research has shown that these two constituencies have systematically different welfare policy interests, with insiders opposed to universal benefit systems when there are large outsider constituencies (Berens 2015). We lack equivalent survey data for the Arab world, but the structural welfare interests of insiders and outsiders are very similar to Europe and are reflected in the organized politics of Arab labor.

3.2.3 Weak and Segmented Organization of Labor Interests

The structural segmentation of labor markets is reproduced in the field of labor organization. Not only are formally recognized unions historically weak and state-dependent in most Arab countries (Bishara 2018; Cammett and Posusney 2010; Hartshorn 2019; Langohr 2014), they also invariably cater to insiders. In some cases, unofficial labor organizations have emerged in parallel to discredited state-endorsed unions. The new bodies often represent formal workers but sometimes also the unemployed. Yet such alternative groups remain weak, fragmented, and unconnected to the informal sector

(De Smet and Malfait 2015; Weipert-Fenner and Wolff 2020). There is no national organization anywhere that specifically represents informal workers – not even in Morocco, the country with the most pluralist union landscape in the region (El-Haddad 2020b, 10). Like in other regions, the informally employed typically are badly organized as their employment is geographically dispersed, they tend to lack a concrete focus for concerted mobilization such as a large employer or a public agency, and are often busy with mere economic survival.

As Figure 16 shows, Arab citizens do retain high material expectations vis-à-vis their governments, with less statist Morocco the only exception. Although the Arab distributive state has been eroding for decades, a strong moral economy persists under which citizens expect government to provide and sometimes refer explicitly to the "social contract" (Posusney 1997; Schmoll 2017; Schwedler 2021).

While in most countries around the world expectations vis-à-vis the state as provider generally decline with education, they stay the same or increase with higher education in the six core Arab cases on which we have data (see Figure 17). This probably has to do with both the weak job prospects of Arab graduates and the history of government promises to the university-educated in particular.

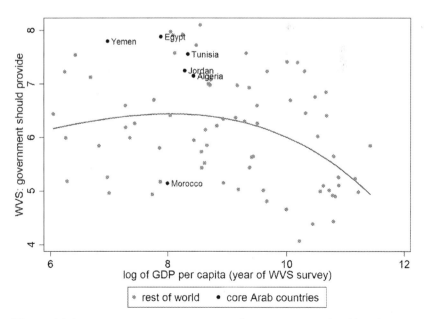

Figure 16 Average agreement to statement that government should make sure that everyone is provided for (1–10 scale)
Source: World Values Survey (WVS), sixth wave.

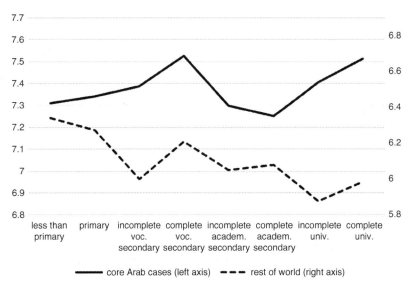

Figure 17 Average agreement to statement that government should make sure that everyone is provided for (1–10 scale), by level of education
Source: World Values Survey (WVS), sixth wave.

When it comes to collective action, however, these high expectations are not articulated through demands for wholesale welfare reform, but either through demands by insiders to preserve their privileges or demands by outsiders to expand such privileges to them. To the extent that there is mobilization in the authoritarian context of the Arab region, it is typically publicly employed insiders who most effectively mobilize against threats to their relative social status such as public employment, salary, or pension reforms (Adly and Meddeb 2020; Weipert-Fenner and Wolff 2020, 18). State workers are the central "inheritors of the old Naser-era employment-based social rights" and have been concentrated enough to collectively organize to defend these rights at critical junctures (Adly 2020, 114 f; Posusney 1997).

Under the pro-market Egyptian cabinet of Prime Minister Ahmed Nazif in the late 2000s, SOE workers and bureaucrats, not the urban poor, were responsible for most of the social protests (Adly 2020, 116). Several authors have argued that the declining status of government employment – a threat to insider benefits – accounts for the disproportionate role of state employees in Egyptian protests before the fall of Mubarak (Beissinger et al. 2015; Kandil 2012). Insiders do have substantial economic grievances, but their articulation in many ways reinforces insider–outsider distinctions.

Even when unemployed or informally employed outsiders protest – usually locally and spontaneously – they tend to demand insider status through government jobs rather than broader welfare reforms, a pattern that has been especially pronounced in Tunisia after the fall of Ben Ali, but is not limited to this case (Han 2021; Schwedler 2021; Weipert-Fenner and Wolff 2020). While rooted in historical regime discourse and practices, this demand for government jobs is arguably boosted by the weakness of the private job market (Assaad and Barsoum 2019). Insider–outsider divisions both influence who protests and which material demands they raise.

The inability to build a coalition that would overcome current insider cartels is quite likely also explained with the persistent authoritarianism in the region, which gives outsiders and rival political elites that could mobilize them less space to organize (Ayubi 1995; Schmitter 1974). Yet at least in the short run, political openings in the region have not led to substantial changes in the insider–outsider systems.

Egypt and Tunisia are the two core cases that have undergone at least a temporary political opening since 2011 and have hence experienced by far the highest levels of political mobilization and, at times at least, freedom of organization and hopes for a new "social contract." I look at these two "most likely" cases for socioeconomic change in more detail to illustrate that even when political constraints are relaxed, organized labor most of all defends insider interests.

Labor Politics in Tunisia

The UGTT in Tunisia is the historically most important union in the region and has emerged as a critical political player after the fall of Ben Ali in 2011.[14] Yet in the field of industrial relations, it has spent much of its political energy since the Arab uprisings on asking for public sector salary hikes (MEMO 2015), fighting government hiring freezes and resisting increases in the formal pensions age above sixty, an issue that has also been a key trigger for mobilizing Algerian and Moroccan unions (El Yaakoubi, 2016; Reuters, 2016). The UGTT mostly represents middle-aged, middle-income insiders in formal employment, the majority of them in the public sector (Hartshorn 2016). In 2014 labor survey data, union membership is associated with

---

[14] The substantial power of the UGTT is rather unusual by the standards of organized labor in the wider Arab world. Tunisia is nonetheless a theoretically important case as the only country with an extended period of electoral democracy after the Arab uprisings. The subsequent Egyptian case study is more representative of the weaker formal organization – yet continued political importance – of insiders.

40 percent higher wages even if controlling for factors like region, gender, age, sector, occupation, and formality.[15]

The union has successfully blocked an IMF deal that would reduce subsidies and public sector employment (Reuters 2021) – expenses for which as a share of GDP are among the highest in the world and which hide thousands "ghost workers" who do not actually show up for their jobs (Bloomberg 2019). The UGTT is less concerned with the numerically larger constituency of informal workers (El-Haddad 2020b) – not unlike established continental European unions which cater to insiders with permanent contracts and tend to ignore the growing number of precarious workers in temporary employment (Dolado 2016; Palier and Thelen 2010).

Precariously employed Tunisian "site workers" with temporary government contracts have managed to extract some local support from the UGTT, but no response from the national leadership, which distrusts their movement (Han 2021). Similarly, a new national union of unemployed graduates formed after Ben Ali's fall has had a tense relationship with the UGTT due to the two organizations' structural competition over state resources (Weipert-Fenner 2020). The new union has been marginalized in official negotiations and has struggled to gain traction among the unemployed population who tend to protest locally and more spontaneously – often with more success as it is easier for government to buy off local protesters with discretionary and limited concessions like new state jobs than to engage in a national, systemic reform process.

When Tunisian outsiders mobilize, they indeed tend to simply ask for insider status to be extended to them: recurrent local protests typically focus on demands for government employment (Weipert-Fenner 2020; Weipert-Fenner and Wolff 2020, 29), with demonstrators in some cases simply asking for one guaranteed government job per family (Gall 2016). Jobseekers left out in public sector hiring rounds have repeatedly staged demonstrations (AFP 2017b). In January 2016, violent clashes broke out in impoverished Kasserine after an unemployed man died when he protested his removal from a list of public sector hires (AFP 2016). In 2017, thousands of protesters in the marginalized southern governorate of Tataouine shut down an oil pipeline, demanding jobs in the local oil industry. The government calmed the situation with a promise of thousands of new state jobs (AFP 2016).

Expanding the ranks of insiders in government employment might function as temporary political pressure valve. But it has come not only at a fiscal cost but also typically at the expense of public sector efficiency. Indiscriminate hiring in the Tunisian health sector has expanded the state salariat but compromised the

---

[15] See footnote 12 for details on the model.

sector's performance (AFP 2017a). Overemployment is particularly rampant in SOEs: in 2021, Tunisair owned twenty-six aircraft, of which only seven were operational, while employing 7,600 individuals – more than 1,000 per functioning plane. The UGTT has resisted all attempts to consolidate the payroll (AFP 2021).

There have been some efforts since 2011 to provide basic welfare for outsiders. Tunisia has expanded universal social assistance tools like the "Programme national d'aide aux familles nécéssiteuses" (PNAFN) cash transfer program and the "AMEN social" cash transfer program, accompanied by an active public debate around universal social coverage. Yet targeting remains weak (Nasri 2020), with an estimated 60 percent of benefits going to nonpoor households in the mid-2010s (ESCWA 2016). A 2016 survey shows that only 30 percent of Tunisian workers were covered by social security (Merouani et al. 2021). Public wage spending, under pressure from insiders and those aspiring to join their ranks, has risen from an already high 10.7 percent in 2010 to an unprecedented level of 17.6 percent of GDP in 2020 (International Monetary Fund 2021a). The increase alone corresponds to more than five times the country's total social safety net spending. While provision for outsiders has improved, the gradient between insider and outsider benefits remains steep. Even the IMF, while scolding Tunisia for its large deficits, has counseled stronger expansion of social safety nets in return for consolidation of the civil services (International Monetary Fund 2021b).

Labor Politics in Egypt

Egypt, like Tunisia, has a long history of state corporatism organized through the Egyptian Trade Union Federation (ETUF), which has mostly represented formal workers, in particular in the public sector. ETUF, however, has enjoyed much less political autonomy than the UGTT, which has led to the emergence of independent sectoral unions just before and after the uprising against Mubarak (Bishara 2018). Yet, all of the independent unions primarily focus on the same formal sector constituencies as ETUF, most visibly the tax collectors' union formed in 2009 as the first organization outside of ETUF. The new unions' primary claim has been to uphold the Nasserist social contract for insiders in government and public enterprises (Bishara 2018; Hartshorn 2019; Langohr 2014).

The window of pluralism in Egypt was brief and President Sisi reestablished authoritarian rule in 2013. Yet labor politics has continued to revolve around defense or expansion of insider privileges. The only presidential law that the tame new parliament under Sisi challenged was an attempt to reform the bloated civil service (Mazen 2016), a proposal that also led to demonstrations of public employees (Jöst and Vatthauer 2020, 90). The parliament eventually approved a watered-down version of the law in October 2016. During the same year, a key reason for the Egyptian government's attempts to avoid an impending currency devaluation was that it would have affected the real income of state employees on nominally rigid wages (Walsh 2016). Once the devaluation happened, the bulk of the May 2017 social adjustment package went into pension increases and civil service bonuses (Wahba 2017).

In Egypt too, political demands of outsiders tend to be limited to asking for the extension of insider privileges: the first public protest in Egypt after the July 2013 military coup focused not on politics but was organized by graduates demanding government jobs (Mansour and Aboelgheit 2016). That said, different from Tunisia, Egypt's unemployed are generally less active in protests (Jöst and Vatthauer 2020, 91), potentially because of their greater social marginality in a poorer country like Egypt.

Like Tunisia, Egypt has made tentative steps toward creating social assistance programs that specifically target the poor and informally employed – a constituency that the devaluation of late 2016 has plunged into particularly deep desperation. Under Sisi, Egypt has introduced the noncontributory cash grant programs *Karama* and *Takaful* with World Bank assistance as compensation for IMF-imposed fiscal reforms. Yet the programs remain small: in 2015, they covered only 5.5 million out of more than 90 million Egyptians (Jawad et al. 2018). This rose to 9.4 million in 2019, which however still represents only 10 percent of a population in which more than a third live in absolute poverty (The Economist 2019b).

The main change in Egypt under Sisi arguably has been the absolute shrinkage of insider benefits through forced economic adjustment, notably through the devaluation of the Egyptian Pound in 2016, which insider constituencies were powerless to prevent, but which hit the material status of outsiders at least as much. While almost no one is doing well in Sisi's Egypt, the difference between material benefits of insiders and outsiders remains steep, and insiders remain comparatively better placed to defend their privileges (see Section 4 for a more forward-looking discussion of Egypt's outlook as bellwether of eroding insider privilege).

The aforementioned case narratives have shown that in both democratic and authoritarian Arab countries, labor politics is deeply shaped by dualism: a significant share of the working population are insiders in the formal sector. Such insiders have a vested interest in state employment and job tenure protections instead of inclusive social safety spending and lowering barriers to employment (Doner and Schneider 2016, 17).

Even in authoritarian contexts, their importance as an established regime constituency exceeds that of the atomized and marginalized outsiders. Their political relevance is reflected in the reaction of both anciens and new regimes during the regional political unrest in 2011. Outsiders were key actors in many of the protests, most visibly in the case of unemployed youth in Tunisia, even if at the peak of economic protests outsiders and insiders often marched together. Devarajan and Ianchovichina (2018) argue that the shortage of formal jobs – the key outsider concern – was a key cause for the Arab uprisings.

Yet across the region, governments in the first instance tried to placate the population by increasing public sector wages and increasing subsidies rather than strengthening more inclusive welfare mechanisms that would benefit outsiders. To the extent that regimes catered to unemployed and informally employed, they did so by creating new government jobs for a minority of them, shifting the boundaries between insiders and outsiders on the margin rather than making their systems more inclusive (Barsoum and Abdalla 2020, 6; El-Haddad 2020b, 10; Han 2021; Hertog 2011; 2021;Langohr 2014, 193; Willis 2012, 258). Even the civil war in Syria seems to only have boosted traditional patterns of distribution: by 2015, five years into the conflict, the number of state employees in Syria had increased to 2.1 million, constituting half of the country's work-force (AFP 2015). The strategy might be politically rational: Mazur argues that Sunnis with access to government jobs in Syria were much less likely to protest during the country's 2011 uprising (Mazur 2021). When insider privileges are secure, they can also explain who does *not* protest.

The status quo of insider–outsider divisions persists because its benefits are relatively concentrated, while the gains of more inclusive welfare are diffuse (Olson 1965). While this is the case with many policies in many countries, in our Arab cases the dynamic is reinforced as (a) the boundaries of insider groups are particularly rigid and (b) they have particularly much to lose. Labor market participants barely face the "veil of ignorance" about their future employment situation that can make more inclusive social security appealing even to the relatively privileged in other countries, for example in Latin American cases (Maloney 2004) and other mid-income countries (Doner and Schneider 2016, 18). Even with limited formal lobbying power, insider interests are therefore highly salient and ruling elites are reluctant to withdraw existing privileges for fear of social unrest.

And while interest group politics remains highly constrained by the region's authoritarianism, insiders have relatively more resources for collective action than outsiders. Outsiders' particularly weak national organization weakens their ability to demand a new distributional regime and engage in more than local, episodic mobilization. State elites are incentivized to privilege relatively better

represented insiders with historically entrenched material expectations, perpetu-
ating a shrinking, state-dependent middle-class coalition.[16] Insider–outsider
divides fundamentally structure labor interest group politics and mobilization,
which in turn help to reproduce material divides.

3.2.4 Summary

In sum, as outlined in the left upper quadrant of the SEME scheme in Figure 1,
Arab labor markets have been deeply divided by ambitious, interventionist
states which cater to a large and sheltered insider group in the public sector.
Privilege is relative – few Arab civil servants live a life of comfort – yet they
remain much better off than the younger majority in the informal sector.
Government funds devoted to a large, if gradually shrinking, insider group
leaves few resources to support the excluded and facilitate their social and
labor market mobility. Outsiders are not well organized and are only capable of
sporadic protest. Relatively better-organized insiders focus on defending their
privileges and have no interest in, or actively oppose, inclusive reform. The
resulting rigidity and durable exclusion on the labor market undermine its
dynamism and lead to misallocation of labor that quite likely hinders productivity growth.

A further factor undermining labor market dynamism and mobility is the
weakness of the private sector, which provides few formal jobs. Like in the
labor market, deep state intervention divides private business into static camps
of insiders and outsiders. Sheltered insider firms, which provide a large share of
private formal employment, lack incentives and capabilities to create high-
quality jobs or recruit meritocratically, and – even more than labor market
insiders – have strong political incentives to defend their privileges. These
structures are discussed in detail in the next section.

3.3 A Segmented Business Sector

In addition to its role as dominant employer, the Arab state also plays a notable
direct function in economic production: some sectors of production in the Arab
world are still dominated by SOEs, including military ones, narrowing the scope
of formal private business. With some exceptions, this role has been declining
relatively fast since the 1990s, however: the inefficiency and subsidy dependence of public industry forced quicker consolidation, and in some cases privatization, than was possible in states' core bureaucracies (Amico and Hertog
2013). In Egypt, Jordan, and Yemen, employment in SOEs now constitutes less

---

[16] See Iversen and Soskice (2012) on how employers and workers in the export sector of European
CMEs can anchor a similar (though more productive) political coalition.

than an eighth of total public employment; in Tunisia it is about a quarter (see labor force surveys cited for Figure 11).[17]

More important for the structure of production in core Arab countries is the division of private enterprises into insiders and outsiders, related to but not identical with the distinction of formal and informal businesses.[18] Such a distinction is not unusual in the developing world, but once again the depth of insider privilege for larger formal players in the Arab world is particularly deep and mobility between segments is particularly low.

One sign of deeper divisions in the business sector is that Arab private sectors are typically divided into some very large firms and numerous small ones, more clearly so than in most other emerging markets (Diwan et al. 2020; Schiffbauer et al. 2015, 29; World Bank 2014, 59; Cammett et al. 2015, 17). High barriers to entry into formal operations are reflected in the very low entry rates for new limited liability companies – the main internationally recognized form of modern formal business – in the five cases where data are available (Figure 18). Companies in the region also remain informal for particularly long periods, again suggesting low mobility from the informal to the formal sector (Devarajan and Ianchovichina 2018; Gatti et al. 2014, 17). Finally, transitions to larger firm size are also relatively rare (Adly 2020; EBRD 2016, 69). Small-scale trading operations and workshops, springboards for formal entrepreneurship in many other regions, typically remain small and informal in the Arab world.

There is, conversely, evidence that once a firm has achieved insider status, it is particularly hard to dislodge. Firms in the Arab region on average are considerably older and fewer firms exit there than in other regions; creative destruction is limited (Benhassine 2009; Gatti et al. 2013; Islam et al. 2022) and large firms are particularly long-lived (Nucifora et al. 2014). Most companies in the region are privately held, as capital markets remain relatively small (OECD 2019), closing the market for corporate control to outsiders. Many of them are multi-generational family empires, making sure privilege is passed on across generations.

Adly (2020, 18) describes the situation in which most small firms fail to become formal or attain credit or land as "economic apartheid." There is little evidence that the dominance of very large firms is due to their efficiency, as one might argue for large conglomerates in South Korea or Japan during their

---

[17] In Egypt, the recent return of military-controlled industries to various sectors of production has reversed the trend of SOE downsizing (Sayigh 2021). Unfortunately, there is no consolidated information about their aggregate role.

[18] Not all formal businesses enjoy particular privileges. We can however assume that practically all informal businesses are outsiders.

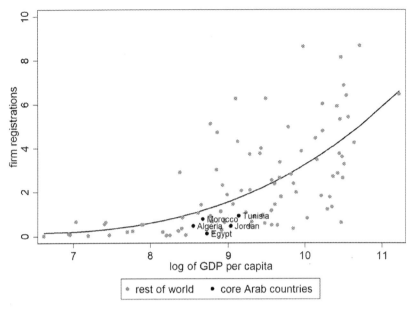

Figure 18 Number of new limited liability companies registered per 1,000
inhabitants (2000–9 average)
Source: Data provided courtesy of Leora Klapper (Klapper and Love 2011).

periods of rapid industrialization. Instead, at least in Egypt, middle size firms
are more efficient than either small or large firms; yet there are unusually few
mid-sized companies compared to other mid-income countries (Atiyas and
Diwan forthcoming).

3.3.1 Drivers of Segmentation

The aforementioned facts evidence insider–outsider segmentation and low
mobility between the segments. The most important reason for this is the state's
extensive and often discretionary involvement in the private economy through
both material support and regulatory intervention.

I have already mentioned the extensive range of material tools – subsidies,
credit, and provision of land – through which Arab states can support private
businesses. All these resources are rationed in practice. Like in the case of
state employment, this makes privilege for some and exclusion for others
inevitable. As important, we have also seen evidence of deep regulatory
intervention in the private sector. There is strong international evidence that
a heavy burden of regulation both reduces firm entry and increases informality
(Enste and Schneider 2000; Klapper et al. 2006). For the Arab world

specifically, Elbadawi and Loayza (2008) have shown that weak rule of law and low regulatory freedom are correlated with higher informality.

There are good reasons to believe that both material support and regulation have asymmetric effects across Arab firms and, moreover, benefit the best-connected or politically most savvy rather than the most efficient businesses. Arab countries rank particularly badly in the enforcement of regulations (Benhassine 2009, 79; Gatti et al. 2013, 18). In all countries bar Jordan, firms polled in World Bank enterprise surveys report above-average impact of corruption on their operations (Figure 19).

Arab countries fare somewhat better on general measures of corruption, such as the "control of corruption" index included in the World Bank Governance Indicators. The high impact of corruption reported by Arab businesses in particular is probably the *combined* outcome of general propensity to corruption with particularly deep state intervention. This is supported by international survey data on tax inspections and bribery, which shows a somewhat higher incidence of bribery *per inspection* in sub-Saharan Africa, but a much higher *frequency* of inspections in Arab countries, resulting in the highest combination of bribery and inspection intensity among all world regions (Gatti et al. 2014, 141).

Unsurprisingly, some firms can navigate this environment better than others. Recent World Bank research demonstrates that the variation in waiting times for

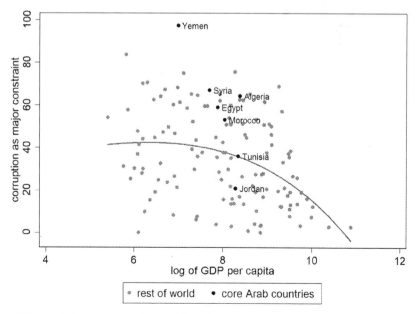

Figure 19 Percentage of firms identifying corruption as a major constraint
Source: World Bank enterprise surveys (most recent years available).

regulatory services in the Arab world is higher than in most other emerging economies (Schiffbauer et al. 2015, 49 f).

Cronyism

Some of the varying ability to handle a heavy bureaucratic environment is undoubtedly due to individual firms' luck, skills, and diligence. But the important role of state resources and deep intervention in markets also create vast opportunities for state–business crony networks, which have been documented in great detail in recent research (Heydemann 2004; Hill et al. 2013; Nucifora et al. 2014). The corruption of politically connected magnates like Bashar El-Assad's cousin Rami Makhlouf in Syria or Ben Ali's son-in-law Sakher El Materi in Tunisia is part of local folklore.

Beyond individual stories, Islam et al. (2022) use international enterprise surveys to find that about 8 percent of firms in MENA have politically connected owners or top managers, a much higher share than in middle-income peer countries. And the impact of cronyism on economic opportunities is larger than their share in the private sector: in Egypt, "politically connected" companies under Mubarak accounted for only 11 percent of total employment, but 60 percent of total net profits among listed firms (Diwan et al. 2020). In Tunisia, firms linked to the ruling Ben Ali family accounted for 0.8 percent of employment but 21.3 percent total private sector profits before the 2011 revolution (World Bank 2014, 112).

Mechanisms for capturing such rents include discretionary access to subsidies, trade protection, credit, government contracts, tax rebates, land, and favorable regulatory enforcements (Adly 2020; Chekir and Diwan 2015; Diwan et al. 2020; Eibl and Malik 2016).[19] Opportunities for administrative discretion abound: the Egyptian General Authority for Investment, for example, regulates entry into the cement and steel sectors, which benefit heavily from energy subsidies and other policy privileges. Entry into tourism or real estate requires acquisition of land and permits to build (Diwan 2021, 41). Diwan et al. found that Egyptian firms in connected sectors on average wait eighty-six days less for their construction permit (Diwan et al. 2020). Licenses in the Tunisian banking and telecommunication sectors are highly restricted and typically reserved for privileged insiders (Diwan 2021, 43). Access to the Tunisian transport sector is similarly limited (El-Haddad 2020b), which is particularly unusual in

---

[19] The detailed quantitative evidence in this section comes from the cases of Egypt, Jordan, Morocco, and Tunisia. Judging from qualitative literature and corruption indicators, cronyism in Syria, Algeria, and Yemen is, if anything, worse (Haddad 2020; Hill et al. 2013; Willis 2012). There is no microlevel econometric evidence on cronyism and its mechanisms, however, as the data situation for these countries is much worse.

international comparison. Across the region, connected firms can benefit from exclusive import licenses (Diwan 2021, 43; Willis 2012, 257). Francis et al. (2018) have shown that the primary business strategy of politically connected firms in Egypt is to sell in protected domestic markets, while comparable nonconnected firms focus on exports.

Credit also disproportionately goes to connected firms, while small companies in particular are starved of finance (Adly 2020). In all, 92 percent of the loans extended to the private sector in Egypt in 2010 went to firms with political links. This bias is both due to the continued heavy (if declining) role of the Arab state in credit allocation (Adly 2020, 76; El-Haddad 2020b, 11; Farazi et al. 2011) and because even private banks see connected firms as enjoying an implicit bailout guarantee (Diwan and Schiffbauer 2018). The politically directed nature of credit allocation has led to high ratios of non-performing loans – peaking at more than a quarter of all loans in Egypt in the mid-2000s (Adly 2020, 137) – which further crowds out credit allocation to productive independent firms.

While cronyism for the largest firms is the most egregious and best documented, informal networks and practices also create forms of exclusion on lower levels. Using a survey experiment on Moroccan and Jordanian employees across firms of all sizes, Kubinec (2018) finds that politically connected firms receive lighter regulation and access to protected markets in return for political loyalty. On lower socioeconomic rungs, cronyism tends to be replaced by coercion: security apparatuses across the region are known for shaking down informal micro-entrepreneurs like street vendors (El-Haddad 2020b, 7), undermining their property rights and development chances, thereby deepening their economic exclusion.

As already alluded, the region's thicket of regulations combined with scarce state resources also brings about some structural, noninstrumental exclusion as even noncorrupt bureaucracies are simply hard to deal with for smaller firms. This again advantages larger incumbent firms; a phenomenon Adly calls "rents without cronyism" (Adly 2020, 193, 195). For smaller firms, the only viable strategy often is avoidance of the state rather than picking fights with bureaucrats, especially in countries with notoriously unaccountable administrations like Algeria or Egypt.

3.3.2 Consequences for Outsiders and for Economic Performance

Politically connected firms and generally heavy administration tend to push the majority of unconnected businesses into unproductive small-scale, often informal activities (Schiffbauer et al. 2015, 82), where they enjoy weak property rights. To the extent we can measure it, the consequences for overall economic performance are dire: Diwan et al. (2020) find that across the Egyptian economy, the distribution of employment in a given sector becomes more skewed toward small businesses after the entry of politically connected firms, reflecting the crowding out of larger, potentially more productive formal competitors. Sectors with politically connected firms also see generally less firm entry.

In Tunisia, historical firm growth has been shown to be only very weakly correlated with profitability and productivity, reflecting high barriers to entry and discretionary protection (World Bank 2014, 65). The dispersion of value added within sectors across the region is particularly high, which also reflects protection and uneven privileges, as we would expect low value-added firms to exit in a competitive market (Benhassine 2009, 103). In Egypt, unconnected firms are seven times more likely to introduce new products than their connected peers, showing how cronyism undermines innovation (Francis et al. 2018).

Visible, high-level cronyism – the quintessential unfair insider cartel – has been a key factor driving unrest across the region since 2010. Top-level corruption of connected business figures like Ahmed Ezz in Egypt, Rami Makhlouf in Syria, or the Ben Ali clan in Tunisia has provided demonstrators from the lower and outsider ranks of society with salient targets (Arampatzi et al. 2018; Bellin 2012; Diwan et al. 2019).

In sum, in core Arab economies, state intervention remains deep and economic opportunities seem to depend more on where a firm started and what its connections are than in other regions, reducing firm growth and mobility into formality, and cementing insider advantages. Such exclusion both keeps smaller firms in informality and creates further segmentation among formal firms of connected and unconnected players. Mid-size unconnected companies are often the most productive yet are few in number and prevented from growing. As firm entry and growth are important determinants of economic growth and productivity (Klapper et al. 2006), such exclusion and low dynamism very likely contribute to the region's underwhelming economic outcomes.

We now have direct sector-level evidence of the anti-growth effects of insider systems: Islam et al. (2022) find that lower market contestability in Arab countries reduces job creation. Diwan et al. (2020) find that sectors of the Egyptian economy into which politically connected firms enter see significantly slower productivity and wage growth compared to sectors that remain unconnected. They also experience slower aggregate employment growth. Without cronyism, employment in the formal sector could have been 25 percent larger in an ideal world of perfect competition (Diwan et al. 2020). This implies that cronyism is an important contributor to the unusually small share of formal private employment that blights Arab labor markets, discussed in the previous section. More broadly, Giovanis et al. (2018) have shown that the bad institutional climate for business across the MENA region, which both facilitates cronyism and makes operations generally harder, has a negative impact on average firm performance in terms of value added and productivity.

The exceptionally low dynamism of Arab business has arguably contributed to weak performance on pretty much all available indicators of economic performance. The Arab world has the world's lowest share of private in total investment and the lowest ratio of manufacturing exports to GDP, which moreover have very low-technology content (Arezki et al. 2019; Arezki et al. 2021; Benhassine 2009, 50, 59, 61). Expenses on research and development are mostly below international levels (see online appendix, Figure O2) and World Bank enterprise surveys show an unusually low use of international quality certification mechanisms by Arab firms (online appendix, Figure O3). The contribution of total factor productivity to growth over the last two decades has been dwarfed by those of labor and physical capital (European Bank for Reconstruction and Development 2013, 12; Rougier 2016). Productivity trends since 1990 have mostly been below those in all other world regions (online appendix, Figure O4).

3.3.3 Weak and Segmented Organization of Business Interests

The segmentation of the private sector carries over into interest group politics. Like for labor unions, deep traditions of state intervention and control have left little space for independent collective action by Arab business. The World Bank describes business associations in the regions as "generally weak, unrepresentative, or nonindependent" (Benhassine 2009, 187). And if they matter, they are dominated by insiders, leaving little opportunity for less well-connected businesses to organize (Benhassine 2009; Malik and Awadallah 2013).

Following the segmentation of the private sector, interests of large and small companies tend to diverge and only those of large ones are formally represented. A World Bank survey of Arab business associations shows that their lobbying typically focuses on the defense of specific insider privileges like regulatory protection and subsidies rather than the broader policy and regulatory reforms demanded by the majority of businesses according to enterprise surveys (Adly 2020; Benhassine 2009, 188). As a result, organized demands for rule of law and for improvements to government effectiveness that could level the playing field and improve firm growth and mobility into formality are weak. This takes reform pressure off government and contributes to a trap of low coordination and low trust in which most companies try to avoid the state rather than cooperate with it (Hertog 2012).

Given the relative weakness of business associations and the prevalence of insider structures and favoritism, businesses often find individual, informal strategies more effective in pursuing their specific interests and dealing with an interventionist state (Hertog 2012; Heydemann 2004). For outsider firms, such strategies typically entail avoidance of the state, while insiders use informal channels to achieve policy change or regulatory discretion in their favor. Recent research on Egypt and Tunisia shows, for example, that politically connected firms under Mubarak and Ben Ali were highly effective at making the state raise barriers to entry in the particular markets in which they operated (Eibl and Malik 2016; Nucifora et al. 2014).

In this context, formal liberalization in one area often just leads to displacement of patronage into others. With the gradual reduction of trade tariffs due to international agreements, for example, the use of NTTBs that benefit insiders has multiplied. By 2010, Egypt had one of the highest frequencies of nontariff trade measures in the world, extending to 147 manufacturing sectors. The share of NTTB-protected products sold by politically connected firms is substantially greater than that sold by unconnected firms (Diwan 2021, 42). In Morocco, sectors with politically connected firms benefited from disproportionately higher nontariff protection after a trade deal with the EU forced an across-the-board reduction of customs rates in the 2000s (Ruckteschler et al. 2019). Monroe (2019) shows that Jordanian firms with ethnic connections to policy-makers are willing to accept formal liberalization measures in exchange for lax tax and regulatory enforcement, uncompetitive government contracts, and access to insider information. When facing the formal opening of markets, well-positioned capitalists use personal connections to trade formal for informal privileges.

In Arab economies, like in European coordinated market economies, businesses use nonmarket, informal coordination mechanisms. But these mechanisms are individualized and typically used for favoritism and individualized bargains rather than for collective policy coordination as in continental Europe. The low investment in technology and skills across our cases arguably happens not only because individual firms are weak, but also because collective business demands for government support in skills and technology acquisition are weak.

3.3.4 Low Social Trust of Insider Businesses

Cronyism, insider privilege, and limited employment creation contribute to low public trust in business. About twice as many World Values Survey respondents have no trust at all in large companies in the region than elsewhere (Figure 20). Scores in the republics again are particularly bad.

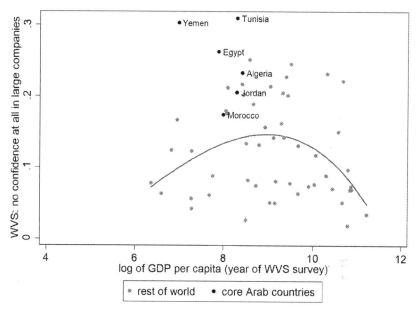

Figure 20 Percentage of respondents with "no confidence at all" in large
companies (WVS)
Source: World Values Survey, sixth wave.

Arab citizens seem to specifically distrust large insiders in business, as
general attitudes to entrepreneurship and markets in the region are positive
(Diwan 2014). While trust in business can be influenced by many factors, Arab
populations' different views about large businesses and entrepreneurs suggest
that high-level insider cronyism is an important part of the story. Distrust in
business elites has been a key driver of protests in 2010 and after (Arampatzi
et al. 2018; Diwan et al. 2019). The most emblematic figure might be Egyptian
steel tycoon Ahmed Ezz, who doubled as key functionary in Mubarak's ruling
party and was a key target of protesters in 2010 and 2011. According to the
New York Times, "Mr. Ezz, in his tight Italian suits, became the best known and
most reviled member of the group around [President Husni Mubarak's son]
Gamal Mubarak," blamed for inflated steel and construction prices as well as
the blatant rigging of the 2010 parliamentary election (Fahim 2011). Protesters
torched his residence in Cairo and he was one of the first senior officials to be
sacrificed by Mubarak in an (failed) attempt to placate demonstrators. Yet after
a few years in prison and an overturned conviction, he has made a return to
Egyptian business under President Sisi, with his business reporting large profits
in 2020 (Billionaires Africa 2021). Crony networks in the Arab world can even
survive revolutions.

Against the background of such stories, low trust in big business is unsurprising. Low levels of trust in turn do little to help encompassing policy coordination between government, business, and labor. As Doner and Schneider point out (Doner and Schneider 2016, 9), trust among stakeholders is needed to form a coalition needed for economic upgrading, as the upgrading process involves complex inter-temporal bargains and promises. The same can be said about the negotiation of a new welfare system that would overcome insider–outsider divisions in the Arab world – if anything, the potential losers and veto players in such a process are even clearer.

To sum up, segmentation of the private sector is another key component of the interlocking features of the SEME scheme (see top-right quadrant in Figure 1): deep intervention of a relatively low-capacity state provides protection and rent-seeking opportunities for larger, often politically connected private players, while smaller outsider firms receive little state support, are often hampered by the government, and try to avoid it. Insider benefits in turn incentivize privileged players to defend or ask for new protection mechanisms, as often through individual lobbying using informal avenues as through collective action. Outsiders, by contrast, have neither collective nor individual access to decision-makers, and therefore no influence on policy and regulation. As a result of this equilibrium, insider status and benefits are remarkably stable, while outsider needs are ignored. Given the salience of insider benefits, social trust in big capital is uniquely low across the region. While the incentives for insiders to defend their benefits are clear, distrust and segmentation of interests make the building of a broader social coalition for inclusive growth a difficult and uncertain enterprise.

3.4 Skills

The last key component of the SEME model is its skewed skills system, which helps to lock Arab economies onto a path of low dynamism and productivity. Segmentation of labor markets and businesses depresses the demand for skills that would be relevant for a diversified private sector. A weak skills basis in turn undermines the mobility of individuals into the formal private sector and pushes them to seek state jobs; it also prevents firms from undertaking technological upgrades and diversification. As I have already elucidated many components of this story from the labor market and firm perspective, this section will be relatively short.

The evidence of low skill levels in the Arab region is strong. As Figure 21 shows, most core Arab countries do worse on standardized test of pupils' abilities than their wealth would predict (Gatti et al. 2013, 24; Tzannatos et al. 2016, 18).

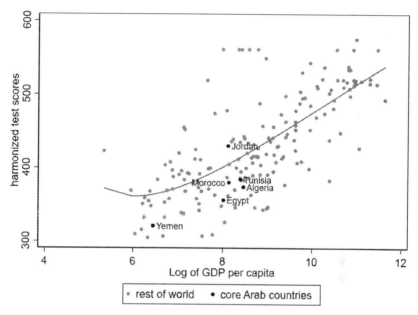

Figure 21 Harmonized test scores measuring student achievement
Source: World Bank Human Capital Index, incorporating a wide range of standardized
international tests.

In the WEF's Human Capital Index, which measures enrolment, the perceived quality of the education system, and skills levels, all cases are within the bottom 40 percent (Figure 22).

This weakness stems from the limited resources available per student and the status of teaching as a secure but often low-status public sector occupation (Brixi et al. 2015; Faour 2012; World Bank 2008b) – itself part of a social contract historically built on indiscriminate government employment. Already in the early 1980s, a disproportionate share of education spending in Egypt went into salaries, contributing to very modest learning outcomes (Waterbury 1983, 219). The rapid expansion of Arab education systems after independence initially expanded economic opportunities. But as the education system has since become a jobs machine like other parts of the public sector, it has become difficult to improve quality. Teachers are in many cases badly selected, badly trained, and underperforming. Like other civil servants, they are difficult to motivate and hold accountable; Arab school systems suffer from considerable absenteeism problems (Brixi et al. 2015; Chapman and Miric 2009; Faour 2012). The teaching profession itself is part of an eroding low-effort, low-return social contract in which teachers are relatively lower-tier insiders.

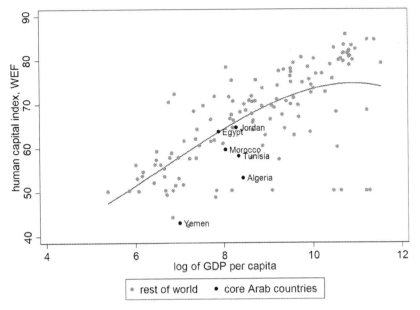

Figure 22 Human Capital Index scores (WEF)
Note: Higher score indicates a better human capital system.
Source: WEF 2016 Human Capital Report.

The deficiency of the Arab skills basis also has to do, however, with the segmented, inefficient, and sometimes nepotistic Arab labor markets, which create little demand for advanced cognitive or practical skills. While government job creation has shrunk significantly, Arab skill systems by and large continue to be organized around public sector-oriented "credentialism," where the formal level of education matters more than the subject studied, as it determines access to government jobs (Assaad 2014b; Salehi-Isfahani 2012; Tzannatos et al. 2016). The perception of the "public sector as the main client of education and training" (Gatti et al. 2013, 25) remains widespread. This is reflected in the excessive focus in tertiary education on subjects of limited relevance for the private economy (World Bank, 2008b). Figure 23 shows the unusually high share of arts and humanities graduates among Arabs with higher education. These subjects are not inherently impractical or distant from market needs. In the Arab context, however, governments have expanded them particularly rapidly, and typically at the expense of quality, because their provision is cheaper than that of STEM subjects, allowing governments to uphold a formal commitment to mass higher education while compromising on quality.

Not only education choices but also job expectations remain shaped by an inherited, if badly fraying, social contract. A 2014 survey by YouGov showed

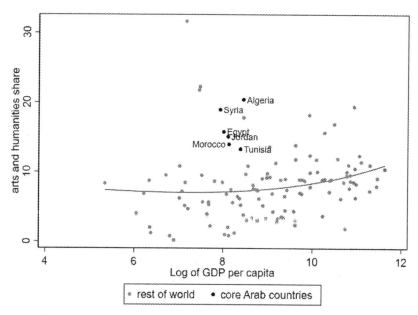

Figure 23 Share of arts and humanities among all tertiary degrees
Source: UNESCO.

that Middle Eastern graduates are only willing to consider a narrow range of jobs, excluding most manual and much service labor. More damningly, the survey report considered 80 percent of them "unprepared" for the workforce (El Yaakoubi 2016). Again, this is unlikely to be evidence of hard-wired preferences or a culture of low achievement, but rather reflects the distorted incentives provided by the local skills system and labor market.

Despite the scarcity of relevant specializations in the government education system, firms in the region for the most part provide little in-house training to compensate for skills deficits (Figure 24). The differences with other regions are stark: Tzannatos et al. (2016, 20) report that while a mere 25 percent of Arab firms provide training, 57 percent do so in East Asia, 53 percent in Latin America, and 40 percent in Eastern Europe.

Enterprise surveys show that Arab firms have a particularly low share of skilled workers in their permanent workforce (see online appendix, Figure O5). The WEF's compound measure for the efficiency of talent use in Arab economies puts all core Arab cases below the international trend line (Figure 25).[20] At the same time, in regional surveys about obstacles to business operations,

---

[20] The measure's components include female labor force participation, reliance on professional management, a country's capacity to attract and retain talent, pay, and productivity.

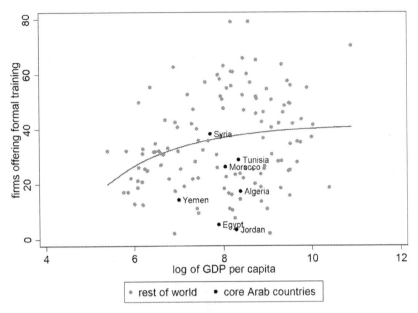

Figure 24 Percentage of firms offering formal training
Source: World Bank enterprise surveys, most recent years.

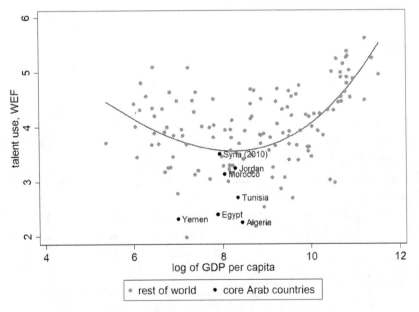

Figure 25 Efficiency of talent use (WEF)
Note: Higher value means higher efficiency.
Source: WEF.

Arab managers tend to rank skills as only a secondary issue. Tzannatos et al. (2016, 17) interpret this as a sign of low demand for skills.

Smaller firms, be they corner stores or family-owned workshops, usually lack the resources to invest in skills-intensive technology. Yet it appears that even many larger Arab firms, sheltered from competition and relying on nonmeritocratc recruitment thanks to their insider status, have made their peace with the low available skill levels, focusing on low-tech production instead of upgrading their workforce.

Weak incentives for skills acquisition are also reflected in low or uncertain returns to education as measured by additional earnings per year of schooling or university: Tzannatos et al. (2016) demonstrate exceptionally low returns to secondary and tertiary education in the Arab world compared to other regions (see also Campante and Chor 2012; King et al. 2010; Montenegro and Patrinos 2014; Rizk 2016). Arab firms are struggling to make good use of more educated individuals, and incentives to seek education are accordingly weak. This disincentive effect is compounded by the role of informal networks on Arab labor markets: Assaad et al. (2018) report that in both Egypt and Jordan family background trumps the quality of education in determining one's time to a first job and one's wages after five years of employment. Arab labor market entrants are often right to lament nepotism and the broken link between hard work and effort (Arampatzi et al. 2018) and as a result give up on skills acquisition.

My own analysis of recent labor force survey data from Egypt, Jordan, Tunisia, and Yemen shows that returns to education tend to be particularly low for informal private employment, the primary (and often long-term) destination of more recent labor market entrants (Figure 26): in all cases, individuals with informal jobs earn less on all levels of education and enjoy lower returns per year of education than those with government or formal private sector jobs. In fact, in the case of Tunisia and Egypt, there is no discernible return to education at all in the informal sector.

Low returns in the informal sector make intuitive sense given the low skill intensity of prevalent informal occupations like taxi driver or street vendor. They imply that long-term labor market outsiders – the bulk of labor force participants, especially among the young – have particularly weak incentives to acquire skills. Low returns are not only economically consequential: the frustration of educated outsiders can also be politically mobilizing. Shafiq and Vignoles (2015) find that the difference between actual and expected educational returns, which according to our analysis is likely to be widest among informal workers, predicts protest participation in the Arab Spring.

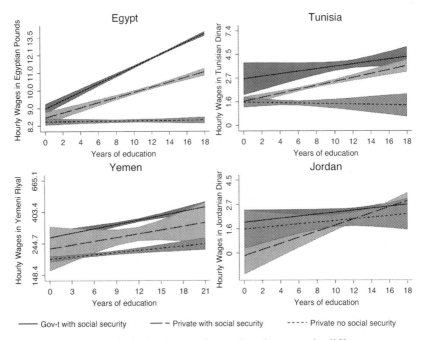

Figure 26 Marginal effect of education on hourly wages in different sectors
Source: See Figure 11.

The picture for the smaller segment of individuals with formal private jobs is more mixed: returns to education are lower than for government employees in Egypt and, marginally, in Yemen – an unusual finding given that private sectors around the world tend to have more unequal pay structures that tend to reward skills more heavily.[21] Returns to education in formal private jobs are higher in Jordan and Tunisia, yet it either takes very high education levels to catch up with public sector wages (Jordan) or even the highly educated in the private sector never reach the average wage levels of their peers in government (Tunisia).[22] All told, we can conclude that labor market segmentation weakens incentives for skills acquisition: payoffs to education are weak both in terms of low returns within most labor market segments and, as we saw above in Section 3.2.1, low chances for outsiders to enter insider segments that offer relatively better skills payoffs.

---

[21] In Jordan, the low education gradient for government workers might be explained with widespread employment in the security sector, where good jobs are available for less educated nationals.

[22] The wage regressions take logged hourly wages as dependent variable and control for age, age squared, urban versus rural residence, gender, occupation and, where available, region/governorate, marital status, and union membership. Models for different sectors are estimated separately. The marginal effects are calculated based on the average of the estimated effects for all observations in the models.

The core Arab world seems to face a particularly bad case of a "low-skill trap" in which limited supply of and demand for skilled labor feed on each other (Booth and Snower 1996; Schneider 2013). Small and rigid formal private labor markets and limited competition among private firms depress demand for advanced skills even more than is the case in Schneider's account of Latin America, giving labor market participants even fewer reasons to acquire them. The resulting weak supply of skills in turn disincentivizes investment into technology-intensive production processes.

Public spending on insider benefits arguably crowds out government spending on training relevant to the labor market. Vocational training systems are weak, badly financed, and considered a dead end by many jobseekers in the region, despite repeated entreaties by international organizations for governments to invest in practical training (Gatti et al. 2013, 24, 178–84). The weak social safety nets for outsiders discussed in Section 3.2.2 make it particularly difficult for jobseekers and the informally employed to invest in skills acquisition as they instead have to focus on economic survival on a daily basis.

Upgrading a skills system is a complex undertaking and requires coordination of many stakeholders (Doner and Schneider 2016, 9, 22). Yet in the Arab world, segmentation and weak organization of business and labor means that there is little coordination between government, firms, and workers on skills formation. Neither insiders nor outsiders have strong incentives to push for skills upgrading. Existing attempts to integrate business in designing vocational training or university programs have been desultory (Ashmawi 2011; Gatti et al. 2013, 177). Vocational programs, generally seen as low quality across the region, hence often miss market needs (Dimova and Stephan 2020). The region lacks a clear coalition for reforming the skills system.

Low prevailing skill levels themselves contribute to the strong demand for government jobs evidenced earlier in the Element, and in practice often leave only informal employment as realistic option, thereby reinforcing labor market segmentation. Workers in secure government jobs have particularly weak personal interest in upgrading the national skills system. Skill deficits make a move toward more inclusive and productive forms of industrial organization and welfare less viable, depressing productivity growth and innovation.

This section rounds off our account of the SEME's interlocking parts. As shown in the lower half of Figure 1, like other spheres of the SEME, the skills system is kept in an unproductive equilibrium organized around insider interests: rigidly segmented labor markets limit incentives to acquire productive skills due to low returns to skills and high barriers of entry to formal labor market segments with relatively better returns. Low skill levels in return make it harder to use the few mobility opportunities that local labor markets offer, further cementing outsiders' exclusion. On the firm side, low prevailing skill levels undermine technological upgrading, thereby keeping outsider firms out. In return, the segmented private sector has only weak demand for skills as outsider firms lack the resources and insider firms the incentives to use them. Firms contribute little to in-house upskilling and have limited interest in collectively upgrading the skills system.

4 Individual Country Outcomes and Alternative Explanations

This Element has presented a wide range of evidence to corroborate our theoretical account of segmented political economies in the Arab world. As expected, the core Arab cases stand out in the degree of state involvement in the economy, the resulting segmentation of labor markets and private business, and a weak skills system that reinforces segmentation. A comparison with averages of nine other world regions in the online appendix (Figure O6) shows that of the sixteen indicators used in the scatterplots, the core Arab cases do indeed have the most extreme average score of eleven, and the second most extreme of five, all in the expected direction. The core Arab cases also score worse than other MENA cases for thirteen of the sixteen indicators.

Where individual country scores deviate from the ideal type, this is consistent with their historical legacies, as it is almost invariably the relatively less historically statist and populist Arab countries that fit the template less well, while populist republics have the most extreme scores. The within-region variation is further evidence for the theory. In Figure 27, I include spider plots that include all of the indicators from the scatterplots used in previous sections and compare core Arab country scores with the global average and the average scores of low- to mid-income countries as defined by the World Bank. All scales are arranged so that a score closer to the center of the plots indicates alignment with the expectations of the SEME model. The post-populist republics Algeria, Egypt, and Syria systematically score on the inside of the plots; Yemen also mostly scores on the inside. The picture is somewhat less clear for Tunisia and least clear for the monarchies of Jordan and Morocco. Yet all of the cases score on the inside of both comparison groups more often than not. Similar patterns for additional indicators are included in the online appendix (Figures O2–O5).

The broad pattern of variation with the region also shows that factors like conflict and natural resource rents (Beblawi and Luciani 1987; Cammett et al. 2015; Heydemann 2000), while undoubtedly affecting Arab development, provide relatively limited leverage in explaining who is more or less

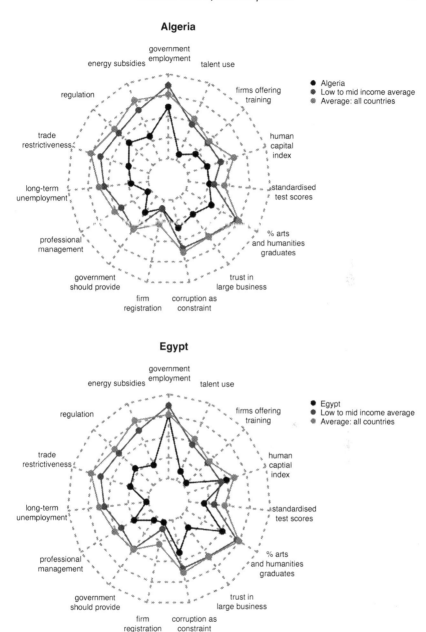

Figure 27 Overview of country indicators

SEME-like: not only are there many conflict-ridden and resource-rich countries in regions like sub-Saharan Africa or central Asia that have developed
very differently from the statist Arab political economies, with less distribution and less intervention, if sometimes more blatant corruption among

Politics of Development

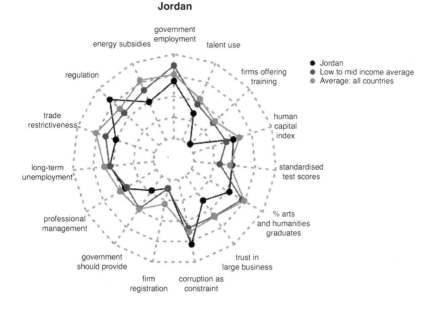

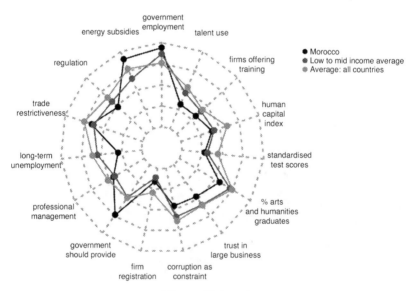

Figure 27 (cont.)

a small elite. Also, conflict and rents do not seem to make countries within the Arab world systematically more SEME-like.

Within the Arab region, cases' proximity to the ideal type is not linked to rent levels or histories of conflict: Egypt has been at peace with Israel since 1979,

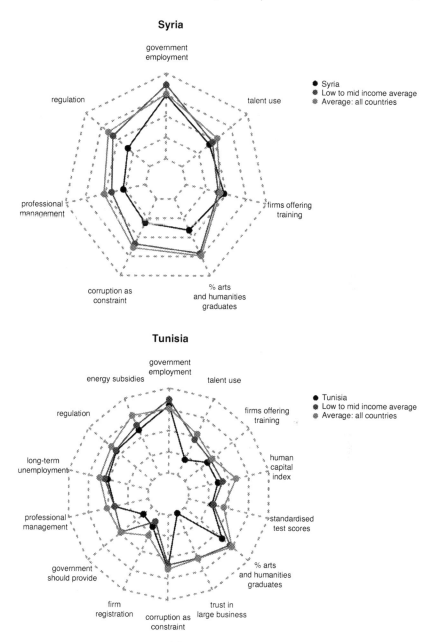

Figure 27 (cont.)

while Algeria has not fought a war since independence, yet both remain the closest to the SEME model. Yemen has experienced more conflict yet fits the ideal type less well. Similarly, external superpower support probably has at times helped some of the cases like Jordan or Egypt to maintain their economic

Yemen

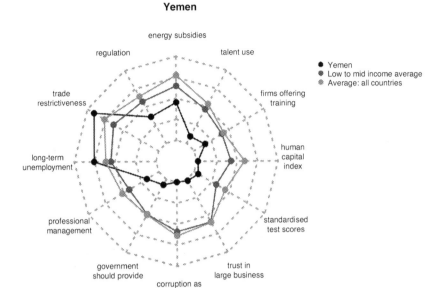

Figure 27 (cont.)

model. But it has not been available consistently (it notably disappeared for Syria in 1990) and does not correlate clearly with SEME characteristics.

And while statism in Algeria certainly is bolstered by hydrocarbons rents, Egypt is similarly resource-poor as Morocco and Jordan, yet a more consistent fit for the SEME type. Finally, the level of authoritarianism, a distinct marker of the whole region, does not seem to make much of a difference, at least not in the short run: as I showed in Section 3.2.3, insiders on the labor market have, if anything, become more entrenched with Tunisia's transition to democracy in 2011. Going forward, should democracy ever spread in the region, this might change: the creation of broader, noncontributory social protection systems in Latin America has coincided with democratization on that continent (Brooks 2015; Haggard and Kaufman 2008). Electoral competition could help political entrepreneurs mobilize outsiders around a less exclusive labor and welfare regime. For the time being, however, the limited political competition in the region seems to have revolved more around (not always credible) promises to enlarge the insider coalition. The biggest signs of change relative to the statist historical legacy have arguably appeared in the one case that has retightened authoritarianism the most after the Arab uprisings: Egypt.

This Element has so far painted a picture of stasis and stalemate. But as economist Herb Stein once said, "If something cannot go on forever, it will stop." The region's resources to protect the region's insider privileges have been dwindling and at some point gradual erosion turns into qualitative change. Egypt, the earliest proponent of Arab socialism and subject to forced retrenchment longer than its peers, provides a glimpse of what this process might look like.

While the Egyptian public sector remains large and the nominal wage bill continues to grow, real government wages have declined since the forced devaluation of the Egyptian pound in late 2016, insider–oriented compensation policies notwithstanding (International Monetary Fund 2019). Such crisis-driven adjustment erodes insider privileges – and has resulted in higher GDP growth rates since 2016 – but it does so through general pauperization rather than inclusion. The social effects of the devaluation, which was in no small measure caused by overconsumption by unproductive insiders, have been brutal. The annual inflation rate climbed above 30 percent. Altogether, the cost of living for average households rose by 50 percent during the devaluation episode and even more for poor households in the informal sector (Alazzawi and Hlasny 2016; Mohamed 2018). According to a study by experts at the American University of Cairo, the share of Egyptian workers deprived of an adequate income has increased from 55 percent in 2006 to 73.3 percent in 2018 (Sehnbruch et al. 2021). At the same time, the Sisi regime stepped up its political repression and criminalized workers' collective action through a new law in December 2017 (Heydemann 2020, 8). While Sisi has made occasional concessions like increases in nominal civil service pay (Arab News 2021; Hertog 2021), the erosion of the old social contract has accelerated under him and has been accompanied by stepped-up repression.

Egypt since 2015 has demonstrated what can happen when the inefficient and resource-intensive dualist Arab model comes under acute pressure from international financial markets. The model's exhaustion in Egypt led to disruptive pauperization through a fiscal and currency shock, which deeply affected insider interests on the labor market, too, and deepened authoritarianism. Given the unsustainable fiscal path of other Arab countries, cases like Jordan, Algeria, or even Tunisia could soon tread a similar path as Egypt.

5 Comparative Puzzles and Gaps

A key objective of this Element has been to put Arab capitalism into comparative international perspective. While the region's empirical peculiarities should be clear by now, they also raise comparative explanatory puzzles and point to gaps in the broader comparative political economy of the Global South. While I cannot fully address these here, I want to propose some hypotheses and directions for future research.

Arab states are not the most corrupt or have the lowest capacity – there are weaker states in some other parts of the world. Core Arab states are instead unique in the scale of their inherited ambitions and obligations relative to their capacity. This might help explain one puzzle that our account of Arab private sectors raises: Why are the economic consequences of cronyism in the region so negative?

The question might seem nonsensical from a neoclassical perspective, where corruption distorts markets and undermines property rights. Yet we know from qualitative work on Asian cases that cronyism does not have to be anti-developmental; it can instead serve as an elite-level coordinating device for growth-oriented industrial strategy (Kang 2002; Wade 2003; Wedeman 2001). More broadly, as Peter Evans points out, it is not usually the depth of state intervention but its quality that matters for economic development (Evans 1995). Why have the types of deep interventions prevalent in the Arab world been so unproductive, leading to almost pure rent seeking for politically connected firms? Why are insiders in the Arab business elites not held to account for economic performance the way that South Korean chaebol were under President Park in the 1960s and 1970s? I would argue that other components of the SEME model work against such performance orientation: first, the bureaucracy is itself too weak and bloated to measure or extract performance – Arab states are employment machines and lack the elite mandarins and autonomous lead agencies that coordinated Asian industrialization (Evans 1995; Haggard 1990; Wade 2003). Second, the market for skills needed for industrial upgrading remains weak and (formal) labor costs high relative to productivity (Kinda et al. 2011). Third, the savings rates and capital expenditure that would be needed for industrial upgrading are crowded out by expenditure on maintaining insider coalitions.[23] Finally, and related to the model's orientation toward domestic consumption by insiders, Arab production by and large is not export oriented, removing a key disciplining device that kept Asian firms lean and competitive (Evans 1995; Wade 2003; Waldner 1999). That all said, the puzzle of cronyism's very different returns in different contexts merits further research.

Conceptually, the reactive nature of Arab policy-making built around insider interests is a key aspect in which Arab states also differ from the new "state capitalism" that has been discussed in recent years with regard to large emerging markets like China or Russia. State capitalism entails the use of productive state assets for purposes of diversification and, in many cases, geostrategy (Bremmer 2010; Musacchio and Lazzarini 2014; Nölke et al. 2015). SEMEs

---

[23] See footnote 9 on debt and capital formation data.

are so caught up in distributional obligations that there is limited scope for long-run economic strategy. They are retrenched, not developmental, or strategic; different from other forms of state capitalism, there is little active industrial policy, and state autonomy is heavily circumscribed. This is a key difference also to the "state-influenced market economies" that Schmidt (2009) identifies in some continental European countries, where the state exerts much more proactive economic guidance. The role of the state in reproducing insider–outsider distinctions also does not figure in theses alternative statist theories.

A second major puzzle is not substantive, but disciplinary: Why is there so little literature on the political economy of labor market dualism in the Global South (Rueda et al. 2015)? Political economists of Europe have developed a rich conceptual toolkit to analyze the politics of insider–outsider divisions that cries out to be tested in the developing world. While dualism is particularly deep and static in the Arab world, precarious informal work is the dominant mode of labor across the Global South and the material deprivation and risks it brings are particularly stark there. We know very little about the political economy of such exclusion and why it is deeper in some cases than others.

The politics of Arab labor evinces many parallels with continental Europe that suggest insights that might be applicable in other regions: established European labor unions tend to represent the interests of permanently employed insiders, often to the detriment of outsiders with temporary (though typically formal) contracts (Saint-Paul 1996). Insiders prefer strong employment protections over flexible regulations that could ease the entry of outsiders into the labor market; outsiders prefer the opposite (Rueda 2007). In 2000s Germany, industrial unions were willing to support the (heavily pared down) noncontributory Hartz IV unemployment assistance scheme as their members were covered by much more generous contribution-based unemployment insurance and not usually unemployed for long. In return, unions received job guarantees and raises for insiders (Palier and Thelen 2010, 18 f.). This closely mirrors the Tunisian UGTT's lack of interest in unemployed, informal, and temporary workers and its preference for insider benefits over broader social assistance.

More generally, the European experience confirms the Arab pattern that labor market outsiders typically lack the resources to mobilize politically (Rovny and Rovny 2017). As in the Arab world, outsiders in Europe tend to bear the brunt of economic adjustment (Rueda et al. 2015). Econometric research on European labor markets has shown that dualism leads to particularly strong wage inequality if collective bargaining is controlled by insider workers (Bentolila et al. 2019). Dual labor markets in Europe are also associated with low total factor productivity growth, poor vocational training, and a large share of small firms (Dolado 2016, 7, 15).

The core Arab world has also followed a similar historical arc as continental Europe: its core social coalition used to underwrite a relatively egalitarian order in the post–World War II era – when European industries were able to absorb most (male) jobseekers on open-ended contracts, and when at least university graduates in the Arab world could all get a government job. The same coalition now underwrites dualism and deep inequality (Palier and Thelen 2010).[24]

While economists and development researchers have examined dual labor markets in the Global South at some length, the same is not true about political economists. How do relatively smaller (and sometimes less securely tenured) insider groups in public sectors in sub-Saharan Africa or developing Asia defend their interests? It is plausible that they are less powerful compared to these regions' relatively larger privately employed middle class, leading to different coalitional dynamics and different forms of labor market regulation and segmentation. Does higher mobility between formality and informality as well as public and private employment create different interests and coalitions? Does it create more inclusive welfare regimes? A comparative investigation of dualisms outside of the OECD, the political drivers of (im)mobility across segments, and the organization of insider interests is of great interest not only intellectually but also from the perspective of social welfare and inequality. This Element is also as a first step toward this global agenda.

6 Conclusion

Core Arab economies stand out in their deep segmentation and low dynamism. I have argued that both are rooted in a history of deep state intervention in the private economy and generous if skewed distribution of resources through public employment and subsidies.

Despite decades of economic retrenchment, heavy state intervention, both formal and informal, continues to the present day and durably divides firms and workers into insiders and outsiders. This static segmentation allows insiders to persist with low productivity (firms) and low skills (workers), giving them a strong vested interest in maintaining a system that allows them to be uncompetitive. Due to high barriers of entry, outsiders similarly have limited incentives to invest in skills. Low skills in turn further weaken the mobility of both workers and firms from outsider to insider status.

The state's maintenance of insider privileges is costly, crowding out inclusive social policies and other investments that could improve human capital and increase

---

[24] One potential difference from European dualism, especially in Northern Europe, is that the privileged core in core Arab economies is particularly unproductive.

labor market outsiders' mobility into formal employment. Segmentation also characterizes the politics of business and labor, in which insider interests tend to prevail. Prevailing low skills and a weak private sector push even outsiders – who are in any case politically marginal – to demand more access to government privilege rather than labor market reforms or a reallocation of state resources toward a modern, inclusive welfare system.

The region's development problem is not simply too much market, as in the conventional leftist view, or too little of it, as in the neoliberal reading. It is instead local economies' very uneven exposure to the market, with excessive protection for insiders on the one hand and brutal exposure to unregulated market forces with threadbare or no social protection for outsiders on the other. This uneven pattern of protection has contributed to the discontent and distrust visible in regional unrest during the last decade or so – both through its generally deleterious impact on economic development and the particular patterns of exclusion it has created.

In the core Arab countries, economic transactions are less market-based than in liberal market economies. Instead, like in coordinated market economies, nonmarket relations and informal networks play an important role, but different from European CMEs these are not embedded in strong meso-level institutions such as unions, employers' associations, or industrial banks. Instead, exclusion, segmentation, and favoritism divide economic actors; undermine trust; and stymie the formation of encompassing interest groups. Agents are left to pursue their interests individually and often through informal means, thereby reinforcing existing divisions.

This Element's objective was conceptual but also to suggest explanations for the low economic performance of core Arab economies. While many other variables likely bear on regional economic outcomes, the interlinked factors of low firm entry, limited formal employment, and low skill formation are bound to exert a drag on economic development via lower productivity. A range of economic studies has indeed linked each of these three factors to low economic growth (Chong et al. 2007; Djankov et al. 2002; Hanushek and Woessmann 2012; Klapper et al. 2006; Loayza and Rigolini 2011; Mincer 1984). Identifying the links between SEME features and growth and diversification with more precision remains for future econometric work.[25]

State failure and inability to deliver basic public goods are worse in some other regions of the world. Yet it seems to be exactly the relatively stronger but skewed presence of Arab states that creates the unique depth and rigidity of

---

[25] One study broadly along these lines is the paper by Rougier (2016), who shows that in the Arab world the interaction of authoritarianism and redistribution (which he calls the "social contract") has a negative impact on economic growth.

insider–outsider divisions in Arab political economies. Perhaps nowhere else in the developing world is the disconnect between state ambitions and state means as deep as in the Arab world. And while there are insider–outsider divisions in many economies, nowhere do they seem to be as deep as in the core Arab world (see online appendix section O6). Parts of the SEME model are likely to be applicable in other regions, but it finds its purest empirical representation in the Arab republics.

There nonetheless are theoretically informative analogies to other world regions, notably continental Europe: similar to Kathleen Thelen's account of continental European economies, the Arab world's core distributional institutions have been rather successfully defended through decades of liberalization, but, as in Europe, the social and distributional consequences of these institutions have changed dramatically and negatively (Palier and Thelen 2010; Thelen 2014). The "institutional drift" (Hacker et al. 2015) of core Arab economies has led to the exclusion of important parts not only of the rural periphery but also of younger, educated urban jobseekers over time. As in Bruno Amable's account of advanced capitalist systems, a dominant social coalition of insiders maintains the institutional configuration of the SEME (Amable 2003), but with particularly strong negative economic externalities.

The system described in this Element has proven resilient even in the face of deep upheaval and political revolutions in the Arab world. As its parts are interlinked and reinforce each other, changing just one aspect is difficult. Adjustment to economic and political crises has happened through shifting boundaries within the system more than changing the system: on the labor market, insider coalitions tend to shrink under fiscal pressure, and occasionally expand as a reaction to bottom-up protests, but the divides between inside and outside remain deep.

This is not to say that change is impossible. The answer to the Arab world's economic challenges however is not more protection and privilege, but a form of egalitarian liberalization in which insiders will have to simultaneously give up some of their privileges to provide more opportunities and mobility, but also more social safety and material support for outsiders. This means redistributing resources rather than just cutting.

The region has seen some discussion about a "new social contract" (Loewe and Jawad 2018), but the debate has remained rather unspecific. Judging by the Latin American experience, Tunisia should have a better chance to create a new distributional regime than most other Arab countries as its more open political system provides more opportunities to organize outsiders around a new, more inclusive economic governance model. Yet even in Tunisia, the political leadership that could provide such a vision has yet to emerge. For the time being,

Tunisia's new-found civic freedoms have most of all benefited well-organized insiders and, at the time of writing, are under acute threat due to President Saied's attack on the country's constitutional structures.

In fact, SEME structures might make democratization more challenging in the region. As we saw in sections 3.2.3 and 3.3.3, insiders and outsider often mobilize separately, with different demands. Even in Tunisia, the much-vaunted civil society behemoth UGTT does not really represent large parts of the population on economic issues. Insider–outsider divides make it easier for authoritarian rulers to play divide and rule, as Al-Assad has done in Syria (Mazur 2021); cronyism in the private sector creates deep-vested interests in regime maintenance; and the low trust between citizens and insider business elites undermines pro-democracy coalition like in 1980s Latin America or East Asia (Haggard and Kaufman 1995).

For all these reasons, a new social contract is difficult to negotiate in the region. An alternative, less fortunate path might be a continued erosion of distribution to insiders due to an ongoing fiscal crisis with no substantive improvement, but rather even deeper economic despair, for outsiders. This is Egypt's current path, at least for its labor market, which unsurprisingly has been accompanied by increased political repression. The political imagination needed to avoid this fate seems largely lacking across the region.

References

Achcar, Gilbert. 2013. *The People Want*. Berkeley: University of California Press.

Adair, Philippe, and Youghourta Bellache. 2014. "Labour Mobility and the Informal Sector in Algeria." TEPP Working Paper 2014–07. TEPP. http://econpapers.repec.org/paper/tepteppwp/wp14-07.htm.

Adly, Amr. 2020. *Cleft Capitalism*. Stanford: Stanford University Press.

Adly, Amr, and Hamza Meddeb. 2020. "Beyond Regime Change: The State and the Crisis of Governance in Post-2011 Egypt and Tunisia." In *Socioeconomic Protests in MENA and Latin America*, edited by Irene Weipert-Fenner and Jonas Wolff, 43–70. New York: Springer.

AFP. 2015. "State Employs up to Half of Syria's Workforce." *AFP*, November 5, 2015.

2016. "Impoverished Interior Poses Risk for Struggling Tunisia." *AFP*, March 2, 2016.

2017a. "Tunisian Public Health Sector Struggles to Heal Itself." *AFP*, May 29, 2017.

2017b. "Tunisia Union Calls for Action against Draft Budget." *AFP*, October 17, 2017.

2021. "Tunisia's Debt-Laden Public Companies Edge toward Ruin." *AFP*, March 7, 2021.

Alazzawi, Shireen, and Vladimir Hlasny. 2016. "Disparities in Cost of Living Changes after a Large-Scale Devaluation: The Case of Egypt 2016." Paper presented at *ERF Annual Conference*. Cairo.

Amable, Bruno. 2003. *The Diversity of Modern Capitalism*. Oxford: Oxford University Press.

Amico, Alissa, and Steffen Hertog. 2013. *State-Owned Enterprises in the Middle East and North Africa*. Paris: OECD.

Angel-Urdinola, Diego, Antonio Nucifora, and David Robalino. 2015. *Labor Policy to Promote Good Jobs in Tunisia*. Washington, DC: World Bank.

Arab News. 2021. "Egypt to Disburse Wage Increases Worth $1.6bn in July." *Arab News*, May 24, 2021. https://arab.news/pt47x.

Arampatzi, Efstratia, Martijn Burger, Elena Ianchovichina, Tina Röhricht, and Ruut Veenhoven. 2018. "Unhappy Development: Dissatisfaction with Life on the Eve of the Arab Spring." *Review of Income and Wealth* 64: S80–S113.

Arezki, Rabah, Daniel Lederman, Amani Abou Harb, Rachel Yuting Fan, and Ha Nguyen. 2019. *Reforms and External Imbalances: The Labor-Productivity Connection in the Middle East and North Africa.* Washington, D.C.: World Bank.

Arezki, Rabah, Rachel Yuting Fan, and Ha Nguyen. 2021. "Technology Adoption and the Middle-Income Trap: Lessons from the Middle East and East Asia." *Review of Development Economics* 25(3): 1711–1740.

Asda'a BCW. 2019. "Arab Youth Survey White Paper 2019." Dubai: Asda'a BCW.

Ashmawi, T. 2011. "TVET in Egypt." Background paper. Washington, DC: World Bank.

Assaad, Ragui. 2014a. *The Jordanian Labour Market in the New Millennium.* Oxford: Oxford University Press.

2014b. "Making Sense of Arab Labor Markets: The Enduring Legacy of Dualism." *IZA Journal of Labor & Development* 3(1):6.

Assaad, Ragui, and Ghada Barsoum. 2019. "Public Employment in the Middle East and North Africa." *IZA World of Labor,* 463.

Assaad, Ragui, Caroline Krafft, and Djavad Salehi-Isfahani. 2018. "Does the Type of Higher Education Affect Labor Market Outcomes? Evidence from Egypt and Jordan." *Higher Education* 75(6): 945–995.

Assaad, Ragui, Caroline Krafft, and Colette Salemi. 2021. "Socioeconomic Status and the Changing Nature of School-to-Work Transitions in Egypt, Jordan, and Tunisia." Presented at *ILR Review Workshop on Labor Transformation and Regime Transition: Lessons from the Middle East and North Africa.* Cornell University.

Atiyas, Izak, and Ishac Diwan. Forthcoming. "Egypt's Missing Middle and Its Impact on Growth." In *The Egyptian Economy: Critical Challenges and Prospects*, edited by Khalid Ikram. Abdingon: Routledge.

Ayubi, Nazih. 1980. *Bureaucracy & Politics in Contemporary Egypt.* London: Ithaca Press.

1989. "Bureaucracy and Development in Egypt Today." *Journal of Asian and African Studies* 24(1–2): 62–78.

1995. *Over-Stating the Arab State.* London: I. B. Tauris.

Barsoum, Ghada, and Dina Abdalla. 2020. "Still the Employer of Choice: Evolution of Public Sector Employment in Egypt." 1386. ERF Working Papers. Cairo: Economic Research Forum.

Beblawi, Hazem, and Giacomo Luciani, eds. 1987. *The Rentier State.* London: Croom Helm.

Beissinger, Mark R., Amaney A. Jamal, and Kevin Mazur. 2015. "Explaining Divergent Revolutionary Coalitions: Regime Strategies and the

Structuring of Participation in the Tunisian and Egyptian Revolutions." *Comparative Politics* 48(1): 1–24.

Bellin, Eva. 2012. "Reconsidering the Robustness of Authoritarianism in the Middle East: Lessons from the Arab Spring." *Comparative Politics* 44(2): 127–149.

Benhassine, Najy. 2009. *From Privilege to Competition: Unlocking Private-Led Growth in the Middle East and North Africa*. Washington, DC: World Bank.

Bentolila, Samuel, Juan Jose Dolado, and Juan F. Jimeno. 2019. "Dual Labour Markets Revisited." CESifo Working Paper. Munich: CESifo.

Berens, Sarah. 2015. "Between Exclusion and Calculating Solidarity? Preferences for Private versus Public Welfare Provision and the Size of the Informal Sector." *Socio-Economic Review* 13(4): 651–678.

Biegert, Thomas. 2019. "Labor Market Institutions, the Insider/Outsider Divide and Social Inequalities in Employment in Affluent Countries." *Socio-Economic Review* 17(2): 255–281.

Billionaires Africa, Editorial. 2021. "Egyptian Tycoon Ahmed Ezz's Steel Giant Reports $152.87 Million in Profit for H1 2021." *Billionaires. Africa* (blog). August 9, 2021. https://billionaires.africa/egyptian-tycoon-ahmed-ezzs-steel-giant-reports-152-87-million-in-profit-for-h1-2021/.

Binzel, Christine. 2011. "Decline in Social Mobility: Unfulfilled Aspirations among Egypt's Educated Youth." 6139. IZA Discussion Paper. Bonn: IZA.

Bishara, Dina. 2018. *Contesting Authoritarianism: Labor Challenges to the State in Egypt*. Vol. 52. Cambridge: Cambridge University Press.

2021. "Precarious Collective Action: Unemployed Graduates Associations in the Middle East and North Africa." *Comparative Politics* 53(3): 453–476.

Blaydes, Lisa, and Eric Chaney. 2013. "The Feudal Revolution and Europe's Rise: Political Divergence of the Christian West and the Muslim World before 1500 CE." *American Political Science Review* 107(1): 16–34.

Bloomberg. 2019. "Haunted by Ghost Workers, Tunisian Phosphate Miner Seeks Revival." *Bloomberg*, November 21, 2019.

Bogaert, Koenraad. 2013. "Contextualizing the Arab Revolts: The Politics behind Three Decades of Neoliberalism in the Arab World." *Middle East Critique* 22(3): 213–234.

Booth, Alison L., and Dennis J. Snower. 1996. *Acquiring Skills: Market Failures, Their Symptoms and Policy Responses*. Cambridge: Cambridge University Press.

Bosch, Mariano, and William Maloney. 2010. "Comparative Analysis of Labor Market Dynamics Using Markov Processes." *Labour Economics* 17(4): 621–631.

Bremmer, Ian. 2010. *The End of the Free Market*. New York: Viking.

Briggs, Biobele. 2007. "Problems of Recruitment in Civil Service: Case of the Nigerian Civil Service." *African Journal of Business Management* 1(6): 142–153.

Brixi, Hana, Ellen Lust, and Michael Woolcock. 2015. *Trust, Voice, and Incentives: Learning from Local Success Stories in Service Delivery in the Middle East and North Africa*. Washington, D.C.: World Bank.

Brooks, Sarah M. 2015. "Social Protection for the Poorest: The Adoption of Antipoverty Cash Transfer Programs in the Global South." *Politics & Society* 43(4): 551–582.

Burrowes, Robert D. 2005. "The Famous Forty and Their Companions: North Yemen's First-Generation Modernists and Educational Emigrants." *The Middle East Journal* 59(1): 81–97.

2010. *Historical Dictionary of Yemen*. Lanham: Rowman & Littlefield.

2016. *The Yemen Arab Republic: The Politics of Development, 1962–1986*. Abingdon: Routledge.

Cammett, Melani, Ishac Diwan, Alan Richards, and John Waterbury. 2015. *A Political Economy of the Middle East*. 4th ed. Boulder: Westview Press.

Cammett, Melani, and Marsha Pripstein Posusney. 2010. "Labor Standards and Labor Market Flexibility in the Middle East." *Studies in Comparative International Development* 45(2): 250–279.

Campante, Filipe R., and Davin Chor. 2012. "Why Was the Arab World Poised for Revolution? Schooling, Economic Opportunities, and the Arab Spring." *Journal of Economic Perspectives* 26(2): 167–188.

Cassim, Aalia, Kezia Lilenstein, Morne Oosthuizen, and Francois Steenkamp. 2016. "Informality and Inclusive Growth in Sub-Saharan Africa." IDS Working Paper 470. Sussex: IDS.

Chapman, David W., and Suzanne L. Miric. 2009. "Education Quality in the Middle East." *International Review of Education* 55(4): 311–344.

Chekir, Hamouda, and Ishac Diwan. 2015. "Crony Capitalism in Egypt." *Journal of Globalization and Development* 5(2): 177–212.

Chong, Alberto, José Galdo, and Jaime Saavedra-Chanduví. 2007. "Informality and Productivity in the Labor Market: Peru 1986–2001." SSRN Scholarly Paper ID 1820879. Rochester: Social Science Research Network.

Choueiri, Youssef M. 2000. *Arab Nationalism: A History*. Oxford: Blackwell.

Collier, Ruth Berins, and David Collier. 1991. *Shaping the Political Arena: Critical Junctures, the Labor Movement, and Regime Dynamics in Latin America*. Princeton: Princeton University Press.

Dann, Uriel. 1989. *King Hussein and the Challenge of Arab Radicalism: Jordan, 1955–1967*. Oxford: Oxford University Press.

De Smet, Bret, and Seppe Malfait. 2015. "Trade Unions and Dictatorship in Egypt." Jadaliyya. August 31, 2015. www.jadaliyya.com/pages/index/22526/trade-unions-and-dictatorship-in-egypt.

Desai, Raj M., Tarik Yousef, and Olofsgård Anders. 2007. *The Logic of Authoritarian Bargains: A Test of a Structural Model*. Washington, D.C.: Brookings Global Economy & Development.

Devarajan, Shantayanan, and Elena Ianchovichina. 2018. "A Broken Social Contract, Not High Inequality, Led to the Arab Spring." *Review of Income and Wealth* 64(s1): S5–25.

Dimova, Ralitza, and Karim Stephan. 2020. "Inequality of Opportunity and (Unequal) Opportunities in the Youth Labour Market: How Is the Arab World Different?" *International Labour Review* 159(2): 217–242.

Diwan, Ishac. 2014. "Entrepreneurs Brief." Manuscript. Paris.

———. 2021. "New Approaches for a Better Understanding of the Political Economy of the 'New' Middle East." Habilitation à Diriger les Recherches, Paris: Ecole Normale Supérieure.

Diwan, Ishac, Adeel Malik, and Izak Atiyas. 2019. *Crony Capitalism in the Middle East: Business and Politics from Liberalization to the Arab Spring*. Oxford: Oxford University Press.

Diwan, Ishac, Philip Keefer, and Marc Schiffbauer. 2020. "Pyramid Capitalism: Cronyism, Regulation, and Firm Productivity in Egypt." *The Review of International Organizations* 15(1): 211–246.

Diwan, Ishac, and Marc Schiffbauer. 2018. "Private Banking and Crony Capitalism in Egypt." *Business and Politics* 20(3): 390–409.

Diwan, Ishac, and Tariq Akin. 2015. "Fifty Years of Fiscal Policy in the Arab Region." 914. Cairo: Economic Research Forum.

Djankov, Simeon, Rafael La Porta, Florencio Lopez-de-Silanes, and Andrei Shleifer. 2002. "The Regulation of Entry." *The Quarterly Journal of Economics* 117(1): 1–37.

Dolado, Juan J. 2016. "EU Dual Labour Markets: Consequences and Potential Reforms." Manuscript. Florence: European University Institute.

Doner, Richard F., and Ben Ross Schneider. 2016. "The Middle-Income Trap: More Politics than Economics." *World Politics* 68(4): 608–644.

Dornbusch, Rudiger, and Sebastian Edwards, eds. 1991. *The Macroeconomics of Populism in Latin America*. Chicago: University of Chicago Press.

EBRD. 2016. "What's Holding Back the Private Sector in MENA?" London: World Bank and EBRD.

Ehteshami, Anoushiravan, and Emma C. Murphy. 1996. "Transformation of the Corporatist State in the Middle East." *Third World Quarterly* 17(4): 753–772.

Eibl, Ferdinand. 2020. *Social Dictatorships: The Political Economy of the Welfare State in the Middle East and North Africa.* Oxford: Oxford University Press.

Eibl, Ferdinand, Neil Ketchley, and Jeroen Gunning. 2022. "Anti-Austerity Riots in Late Developing States: Evidence from the 1977 Egyptian Bread Intifada." Draft Paper. Oxford.

Eibl, Ferdinand, and Adeel Malik. 2016. "The Politics of Partial Liberalization: Cronyism and Non-Tariff Protection in Mubarak's Egypt." Manuscript. Oxford.

Elbadawi, Ibrahim, and Norman Loayza. 2008. "Informality, Employment and Economic Development in the Arab World." *Journal of Development and Economic Policies* 10(2): 25–75.

El-Gammal, Yasser. 2013. "Can the Arab Awakening Change an Entrenched Culture of Nepotism?" Voices and Views: Middle East and North Africa. April 29, 2013. http://blogs.worldbank.org/arabvoices/can-arab-awakening-change-entrenched-culture-nepotism.

El-Haddad, Amirah. 2020a. "Redefining the Social Contract in the Wake of the Arab Spring: The Experiences of Egypt, Morocco and Tunisia." *World Development* 127: 104774.

El-Meehy, Asya. 2010. *Rewriting the Social Contract: The Social Fund and Egypt's Politics of Retrenchment.* Toronto: University of Toronto.

El-Said, Hamed, and Jane Harrigan. 2009. "'You Reap What You Plant': Social Networks in the Arab World—The Hashemite Kingdom of Jordan." *World Development* 37(7): 1235–1249.

El Yaakoubi, Aziz. 2016. "Morocco Upper House Approves Draft Bill on Pension Reform." *Reuters*, June 29, 2016.

Enste, Dominik H., and Friedrich Schneider. 2000. "Shadow Economies: Size, Causes, and Consequences." *Journal of Economic Literature* 38(1): 77–114.

ESCWA. 2016. "Social Protection Country Profile: Tunisia." Beirut: Economic and Social Commission for Western Asia.

2020. "Social Protection Reform in Arab Countries." Beirut: United Nations Economic and Social Commission for Western Asia.

European Bank for Reconstruction and Development. 2013. "Stuck in Transition?" Transition Report. London: EBRD.

Evans, Peter B. 1995. *Embedded Autonomy.* Princeton: Princeton University Press.

Fahim, Kareen. 2011. "Egypt's Ire Turns to Confidant of Mubarak's Son." *New York Times*, February 6, 2011.

Falco, Paolo, and Francis Teal. 2012. "Unemployment, Not Working and Jobs for the Young in Urban Africa: Evidence from Ghana." Oxford: Centre for the Study of African Economies.

Faour, Muhammad. 2012. "The Arab World's Education Report Card." Carnegie Papers. Washington, DC: Carnegie Endowment.

Farazi, Subika Feyen, Erik, and Rocha, Roberto. 2011. *Bank Ownership and Performance in the Middle East and North Africa Region*. Policy Research Working Papers. World Bank. https://doi.org/10.1596/1813-9450-5620.

Feldmann, Magnus. 2019. "Global Varieties of Capitalism." *World Politics* 71(1): 162–196.

Ferrali, Romain. 2012. "The Maghribi Industrialists: Contract Enforcement in the Moroccan Industry, 1956-82." 169/12. Economic History Working Papers. London: London School of Economics.

Filho, Fernando. 2012. "Income Inequality and Labor Market Dynamics in Brazil." Rio de Janeiro: Fundação Getulio Vargas.

Francis, David, Sahar Hussain, and Marc Schiffbauer. 2018. "Do Politically Connected Firms Innovate, Contributing to Long-Term Economic Growth?" 8502. Policy Research Working Paper. Washington, DC: World Bank.

Gall, Carlotta. 2016. "Tunisian Town Simmers with Unrest." *New York Times*, February 8, 2016.

Galli, Rossana, and David Kucera. 2004. "Labor Standards and Informal Employment in Latin America." *World Development* 32(5): 809–828.

Gatti, Roberta, Diego Angel-Urdinola, Joana Silva, and Andras Bodor. 2014. *Striving for Better Jobs: The Challenge of Informality in the Middle East and North Africa*. Washington, DC: World Bank.

Gatti, Roberta, Matteo Morgandi, and Rebekka Grun. 2013. *Jobs for Shared Prosperity: Time for Action in the Middle East and North Africa*. Washington, DC: World Bank.

Ghaith, Zuraiqat, and Hadeel Abu Shama. 2015. "Social Protection and Safety Nets in Jordan." Bristol and Rome: Institute of Development Studies and World Food Program.

Giovanis, Eleftherios, and Oznur Ozdamar. 2018. "The Nexus between Business-Investment Climate and Firm Performance in the Middle East and North Africa (MENA) Region." 1277. ERF Working Papers. Cairo: Economic Research Forum.

Guazzone, Laura, and Daniela Pioppi, eds. 2009. *The Arab State and Neo-Liberal Globalization*. Reading: Ithaca Press.

Hacker, Jacob S., Kathleen Thelen, and Paul Pierson. 2015. "Drift and Conversion: Hidden Faces of Institutional Change." In *Advances in Comparative-Historical Analysis*, edited by James Mahoney and Kathleen Thelen, 180–208. Cambridge: Cambridge University Press.

Haddad, Bassam. 2020. *Business Networks in Syria*. Stanford: Stanford University Press.

Haggard, Stephan. 1990. *Pathways from the Periphery: The Politics of Growth in the Newly Industrializing Countries*. Ithaca: Cornell University Press.

Haggard, Stephan, and Robert R. Kaufman. 1995. *The Political Economy of Democratic Transitions* Princeton: Princeton University Press.

2008. *Development, Democracy, and Welfare States*. Princeton: Princeton University Press.

Hall, Peter A., and David W. Soskice, eds. 2001. *Varieties of Capitalism: The Institutional Foundations of Comparative Advantage*. Oxford: Oxford University Press.

Han, Saerom. 2021. "Resisting State-Produced Precarity through Collective Actions." Paper presented at *ILR Review Workshop on Labor Transformation and Regime Transition: Lessons from the Middle East and North Africa*. Cornell University.

Hancké, Bob, Martin Rhodes, and Mark Thatcher, eds. 2007. *Beyond Varieties of Capitalism*. Oxford: Oxford University Press.

Hansen, Brent, and Karim Nashashibi. 1975. "Foreign Trade in the Egyptian Economy." In *Foreign Trade Regimes and Economic Development: Egypt*, edited by Brent Hansen and Karim Nashashibi, 3–24. Cambridge, Mass.: NBER.

Hanushek, Eric A., and Ludger Woessmann. 2012. "Do Better Schools Lead to More Growth?" *Journal of Economic Growth* 17(4): 267–321.

Hartshorn, Ian. 2016. "Tunisia's Labor Union Won the Nobel Peace Prize. But Can It Do Its Job?" *Monkey Cage* (blog). February 26, 2016. www.washingtonpost.com/news/monkey-cage/wp/2016/02/26/tunisias-labor-union-won-the-nobel-peace-prize-but-can-it-do-its-job/?utm_term=.38549925aff4.

2019. *Labor Politics in North Africa: After the Uprisings in Egypt and Tunisia*. Cambridge: Cambridge University Press.

Haut Commissariat au Plan, Moroc. 2013. "Activité, Emploi et Chômage 2013." Rabat: Direction de la Statistique.

Henry, Clement M., and Robert Springborg. 2010. *Globalization and the Politics of Development in the Middle East*. 2nd ed. Cambridge: Cambridge University Press.

Hertog, Steffen. 2011. "The Perils of Economic Populism in the Mideast." *Bloomberg*, July 25, 2011. www.bloomberg.com/news/articles/2011-07-07/perils-of-economic-populism-in-the-mideast-commentary-by-steffen-hertog.

2012. "The Role of MENA Business in Policy-Making and Political Transitions." In *Business Politics in the Middle East*, edited by Steffen Hertog, Giacomo Luciani, and Marc Valeri, 1–16. London: Hurst.

2014. "Rent Distribution, Labour Markets and Development in High-Rent Countries." LSE Kuwait Programme Paper Series (40). London: LSE.

2021. "When Rentier Patronage Breaks Down: The Politics of Citizen Outsiders on Gulf Oil States' Labor Markets." Paper presented at *ILR Review Workshop on Labor Transformation and Regime Transition: Lessons from the Middle East and North Africa*. Cornell University.

Heydemann, Steven. 1999. *Authoritarianism in Syria: Institutions and Social Conflict, 1946–1970*. Ithaca: Cornell University Press.

ed. 2000. *War, Institutions, and Social Change in the Middle East*. Berkeley: University of California Press.

ed. 2004. *Networks of Privilege in the Middle East*. London: Palgrave Macmillan.

2007. *Upgrading Authoritarianism in the Arab World*. Saban Center Analysis Paper. Washington, DC: Brookings Institution.

2020. "Rethinking Social Contracts in the MENA Region: Economic Governance, Contingent Citizenship, and State-Society Relations after the Arab Uprisings." *World Development* 135: 105019.

Hill, Ginny, Peter Salisbury, Léonie Northedge, and Jane Kinninmont. 2013. "Yemen: Corruption, Capital Flight and Global Drivers of Conflict." Chatham House Report. London: Chatham House.

Hinnebusch, Raymond A. 1985. *Egyptian Politics under Sadat: The Post-Populist Development of an Authoritarian-Modernizing State*. Cambridge: Cambridge University Press.

1989. *Peasant and Bureaucracy in Ba'thist Syria: The Political Economy of Rural Development*. Boulder: Westview Press.

1997. "Syria: The Politics of Economic Liberalisation." *Third World Quarterly* 18(2): 249–266.

2004. *Syria: Revolution from Above*. Abingdon: Routledge.

IADB. 2004. *Good Jobs Wanted: Labor Markets in Latin America*. Washington, DC: Inter-American Development Bank.

International Monetary Fund. 2019. "Egypt: Fourth Review Under the Extended Arrangement Under the Extended Fund Facility." Country Report 19/98. Washington, DC: International Monetary Fund.

2021a. "Morocco: 2021 Article IV Consultation – Staff Report." Country Report 21/2. Washington, DC: International Monetary Fund.

2021b. "Tunisia: 2021 Article IV Consultation – Staff Report." Country Report 21/44. Washington, DC: International Monetary Fund.

Intini, Vito. 2021. "Informality in the Arab Region." Presented at the Social Policy in the MENA Region amid the Pandemic, Doha: HBK University, April.

Islam, Asif, Dalal Moosa, and Federica Saliola. 2022. *Jobs Undone: Reshaping the Role of the Governments toward Markets and Workers in the Middle East and North Africa*. Washington, DC: World Bank.

Iversen, Torben, and David Soskice. 2012. "Modern Capitalism and the Advanced Nation State: Understanding the Causes of the Crisis." In *Coping with Crisis: Government Reactions to the Great Recession*, edited by Nancy Bermeo and Jonas Pontusson, 35–64. New York: Russell Sage Foundation.

Jawad, Rana. 2015. "Social Protection and Social Policy Systems in the MENA Region." New York: UNDESA.

Jawad, Rana, Nora Aboushady, Hicham Ait Mansour et al. 2018. "New Directions in Social Policy in MENA Region." Geneva: United Nations Research Institute for Social Development.

Jebari, Idriss. 2020. "Ben Salah and the Fate of Destourian Socialism in Tunisia in the 1960s." *Jadaliyya* (blog). September 23, 2020. www.jadaliyya.com/Details/41752.

Joffe, George. 1988. "Morocco: Monarchy, Legitimacy and Succession." *Third World Quarterly* 10(1): 201–228.

Jöst, Prisca, and Jan-Philipp Vatthauer. 2020. "Socioeconomic Contention in Post-2011 Egypt and Tunisia: A Comparison." In *Socioeconomic Protests in MENA and Latin America*, edited by Irene Weipert-Fenner and Jonas Wolff, 71–103. New York: Springer.

Joya, Angela. 2007. "Syria's Transition, 1970–2005: From Centralization of the State to Market Economy." In *Transitions in Latin America and in Poland and Syria*, edited by Paul Zarembka, 163–201. Bingley: Emerald Group.

2017. "Neoliberalism, the State and Economic Policy Outcomes in the Post-Arab Uprisings: The Case of Egypt." *Mediterranean Politics* 22(3): 339–361.

Jreisat, Jamil E. 1989. "Bureaucracy and Development in Jordan." *Journal of Asian and African Studies* 24(1–2): 94–105.

Kaboub, Fadhel. 2013. "The End of Neoliberalism? An Institutional Analysis of the Arab Uprisings." *Journal of Economic Issues* 47(2): 533–544.

Kandil, Hazem. 2012. "Why Did the Egyptian Middle Class March to Tahrir Square?" *Mediterranean Politics* 17(2): 197–215.

Kang, David C. 2002. *Crony Capitalism: Corruption and Development in South Korea and the Philippines*. Cambridge: Cambridge University Press.

Kavuma, Kavuma, Oliver Morrisey, and Richard Upward. 2015. "Worker Flows and the Impact of Labour Transitions on Earnings in Uganda." CREDIT Research Paper 15/01. Nottingham: Centre for Research in Economic Development and International Trade.

Kee, Hiau Looi, Alessandro Nicita, and Marcelo Olarreaga. 2009. "Estimating Trade Restrictiveness Indices." *Economic Journal* 119(534): 172–199.

Kerr, Malcolm. 1965. *The Arab Cold War, 1958–1964*. Oxford: Oxford University Press.

Kienle, Eberhard. 1990. *Ba'th v. Ba'th: The Conflict Between Syria and Iraq, 1968–1989*. London: I. B. Tauris.

Kinda, Tidiane, Patrick Plane, and Marie-Ange Véganzonès-Varoudakis. 2011. "Firm Productivity and Investment Climate in Developing Countries: How Does Middle East and North Africa Manufacturing Perform?" *The Developing Economies* 49(4): 429–462.

King, Elizabeth M., Claudio E. Montenegro, and Peter F. Orazem. 2010. "Economic Freedom, Human Rights, and the Returns to Human Capital: An Evaluation of the Schultz Hypothesis." 320. Working Papers. University of Chile, Department of Economics.

King, Stephen J. 2009. *The New Authoritarianism in the Middle East and North Africa*. Bloomington: Indiana University Press.

Klapper, Leora, and Inessa Love. 2011. "The Impact of the Financial Crisis on New Firm Registration." *Economics Letters* 113(1): 1–4.

Klapper, Leora, Luc Laeven, and Raghuram Rajan. 2006. "Entry Regulation as a Barrier to Entrepreneurship." *Journal of Financial Economics* 82(3): 591–629.

Kubinec, Robert. 2018. "Patrons or Clients? Measuring and Experimentally Evaluating Political Connections of Firms in Morocco and Jordan." 1280. ERF Working Papers. Economic Research Forum.

Kuran, Timur. 2012. *The Long Divergence*. Princeton University Press.

Lackner, Helen. 1985. *PDR Yemen: Outpost of Socialist Development in Arabia*. Reading: Ithaca Press.

Langohr, Vickie. 2014. "Labor Movements and Organizations." In *The Arab Uprisings Explained*, edited by Marc Lynch, 180–200. New York: Columbia University Press.

Levin, Victoria, Joana Silva, and Matteo Morgandi. 2012. *Inclusion and Resilience: The Way Forward for Social Safety Nets in the Middle East and North Africa*. Washington, DC: World Bank.

Loayza, Norman V., and Jamele Rigolini. 2011. "Informal Employment: Safety Net or Growth Engine?" *World Development* 39(9): 1503–1515.

Loewe, Markus. 2010. *Soziale Sicherung in den arabischen Ländern*. Baden-Baden: Nomos.

Loewe, Markus, and Rana Jawad. 2018. "Introducing Social Protection in the Middle East and North Africa: Prospects for a New Social Contract?" *International Social Security Review* 71(2): 3–18.

Malik, Adeel, and Bassem Awadallah. 2013. "The Economics of the Arab Spring." *World Development* 45: 296–313.

Malley, Robert. 1996. *The Call from Algeria: Third Worldism, Revolution, and the Turn to Islam*. Berkeley: University of California Press.

Maloney, William. 1999. "Does Informality Imply Segmentation in Urban Labor Markets?" *The World Bank Economic Review* 13(2): 275–302.
2004. "Informality Revisited." *World Development* 32(7): 1159–1178.

Manacorda, Marco, Furio Camillo Rosati, Marco Ranzani, and Giuseppe Dachille. 2017. "Pathways from School to Work in the Developing World." *IZA Journal of Labor & Development* 6(1).

Mansour, Abdelrahman, and Mohamed Aboelgheit. 2016. "Hope without Illusion: Ten Signs of Change in Egypt." Jadaliyya. March 14, 2016. www.jadaliyya.com/pages/index/24060/hope-without-illusion_ten-signs-of-change-in-egypt.

Mazen, Maram. 2016. "Egypt's 'Milestone' Parliament Criticized as Rubber Stamp." *AFP*, October 10, 2016.

Mazur, Kevin. 2021. *Revolution in Syria: Identity, Networks, and Repression*. Cambridge Studies in Comparative Politics. Cambridge: University Press.

McLaughlin, Gerald T. 1978. "Infitah in Egypt: An Appraisal of Egypt's Open-Door Policy for Foreign Investment." *Fordham Law Review* 46(5): 885–906.

MEMO. 2015. "Tunisian Government Raises Public Sector Salaries." *Middle East Monitor*, September 23, 2015. www.middleeastmonitor.com/news/africa/21242-tunisian-government-raises-public-sector-salaries.

Merouani, Walid, Claire El Moudden, and Nacer Eddine Hammouda. 2021. "Social Security Enrollment as an Indicator of State Fragility and Legitimacy: A Field Experiment in Maghreb Countries." *Social Sciences* 10(7).

Mincer, Jacob. 1984. "Human Capital and Economic Growth." *Economics of Education Review* 3(3): 195–205.

Mitchell, Timothy. 1999. "Dreamland: The Neoliberalism of Your Desires." *Middle East Report* 210: 28–33.

Mohamed, Hasnaa. 2018. "2 Years Later, How Have People's Lives Been Impacted by the Flotation of the Egyptian Pound?" Mada Masr. November 18, 2018. www.madamasr.com/en/2018/11/05/feature/econ omy/two-years-later-how-have-peoples-lives-been-impacted-by-the-flota tion-of-the-egyptian-pound/.

Monga, Celestin, and Justin Yifu Lin. 2015. *The Oxford Handbook of Africa and Economics*. Oxford: Oxford University Press.

Monroe, Steve L. 2019. "Varieties of Protectionism: Ethnic Politics and Business Politics in Jordan." In *Crony Capitalism in the Middle East*, edited by Izak Atiyas, Ishac Diwan, and Adeel Malik, 263–88. Oxford: Oxford University Press.

Montenegro, Claudio E., and Harry A. Patrinos. 2014. "Comparable Estimates of Returns to Schooling around the World." 7020. Policy Research Working Paper Series. Washington, DC: World Bank.

Mufti, Malik. 1996. *Sovereign Creations: Pan-Arabism and Political Order in Syria and Iraq*. Ithaca: Cornell University Press.

Murphy, Emma. 1999. *Economic and Political Change in Tunisia*. New York: Springer.

Musacchio, Aldo, and Sérgio G. Lazzarini. 2014. *Reinventing State Capitalism: Leviathan in Business, Brazil and Beyond*. Harvard: Harvard University Press.

Musingafi, Maxwell, Emmanuel Dumub, and Patrick Chadomoyo. 2013. "Improving Performance in the African Civil Service: Empirical Evidence from Zimbabwe." *Public Policy and Administration Research* 3(3): 19–26.

Nasri, Khaled. 2020. "Social Safety Nets in Tunisia: Do Benefits Reach the Poor and Vulnerable Households at the Regional Level?" GLO Discussion Paper.

Niu, Zhaohui, Chang Liu, Saileshsingh Gunessee, and Chris Milner. 2018. "Non-Tariff and Overall Protection: Evidence across Countries and over Time." *Review of World Economics* 154(4): 675–703.

Nölke, Andreas, and Arjan Vliegenthart. 2009. "Enlarging the Varieties of Capitalism: The Emergence of Dependent Market Economies in East Central Europe." *World Politics* 61(4): 670–702.

Nölke, Andreas, and Simone Claar. 2013. "Varieties of Capitalism in Emerging Economies." *Transformation: Critical Perspectives on Southern Africa* 81(1): 33–54.

Nölke, Andreas, Tobias ten Brink, Simone Claar, and Christian May. 2015. "Domestic Structures, Foreign Economic Policies and Global Economic

Order: Implications from the Rise of Large Emerging Economies." *European Journal of International Relations* 21(3): 538–567.

Nucifora, Antonio, Bob Rijkers, and Caroline Freund. 2014. "All in the Family: State Capture in Tunisia." 6810. Policy Research Working Papers. Washington, DC: World Bank.

OECD. 2013. "Pensions at a Glance Asia/Pacific." Paris: OECD.

——— 2014. "Government at a Glance: Latin American and the Caribbean." Paris: OECD.

——— 2019. *Corporate Governance in MENA*. Paris: OECD.

Olson, Mancur. 1965. *The Logic of Collective Action*. Cambridge: Harvard University Press.

Osorio, Rafael Guerreiro, and Fábio Veras Soares. 2017. "Social Protection after the Arab Spring." Policy in Focus. Brasilia: International Policy Centre for Inclusive Growth.

Owen, Roger, and Şevket Pamuk. 1998. *A History of Middle East Economies in the Twentieth Century*. London: I. B. Tauris.

Packard, Truman, and Trang Van Nguyen. 2014. *East Asia Pacific at Work: Employment, Enterprise, and Well-Being*. Washington, DC: World Bank.

Palier, Bruno, and Kathleen Thelen. 2010. "Institutionalizing Dualism: Complementarities and Change in France and Germany." *Politics & Society* 38(1): 119–148.

Peters, Anne Mariel, and Pete W. Moore. 2009. "Beyond Boom and Bust: External Rents, Durable Authoritarianism, and Institutional Adaptation in the Hashemite Kingdom of Jordan." *Studies in Comparative International Development* 44(3): 256–285.

Pierson, Paul. 2000. "Increasing Returns, Path Dependence, and the Study of Politics." *The American Political Science Review* 94(2): 251–267.

Pieterson, C. 2014. "Employee Turnover in a Local Government Department." *Mediterranean Journal of Social Sciences* 5(2): 141–153.

Posusney, Marsha Pripstein. 1997. *Labor and the State in Egypt: Workers, Unions, and Economic Restructuring*. New York: Columbia University Press.

Ramachandran, S. 2004. "Economic Development in the 1990s and Jordan: World Bank Assistance." Country Assistance Evaluation 82103. Country Assistance Evaluation. Washington, DC: World Bank.

Reuters. 2016. "Political Rifts Threaten Tunisia Economic Reform." *Reuters*, April 30, 2016.

——— 2021. "Analysis: Tunisian Political Chaos Threatens IMF Deal." *Reuters*, May 27, 2021.

Rizk, Reham. 2016. "Returns to Education: An Updated Comparison from Arab Countries." 986. ERF Working Papers. Economic Research Forum.

Robalino, David. 2005. *Pensions in the Middle East and North Africa: Time for Change*. Washington, DC: World Bank.

Robins, Philip. 2004. *A History of Jordan*. Cambridge: Cambridge University Press.

Rougier, Eric. 2016. "'Fire in Cairo': Authoritarian–Redistributive Social Contracts, Structural Change, and the Arab Spring." *World Development* 78: 148–171.

Rovny, Allison E., and Jan Rovny. 2017. "Outsiders at the Ballot Box: Operationalizations and Political Consequences of the Insider–Outsider Dualism." *Socio-Economic Review* 15(1): 161–185.

Rubin, Jared. 2017. *Rulers, Religion, and Riches: Why the West Got Rich and the Middle East Did Not*. Cambridge: Cambridge University Press.

Ruckteschler, Christian, Adeel Malik, and Ferdinand Eibl. 2019. "The Politics of Trade Protection: Evidence from an EU-Mandated Tariff Liberalization in Morocco." 1352. Working Papers. Economic Research Forum.

Rudra, Nita. 2007. "Welfare States Dn Developing Countries: Unique or Universal?" *Journal of Politics* 69(2): 378–396.

Rueda, David. 2007. *Social Democracy inside out: Partisanship and Labor Market Policy in Advanced Industrialized Democracies*. Oxford: Oxford University Press.

Rueda, David, Erik Wibbels, and Melina Altamirano. 2015. "The Origins of Dualism." In *The Politics of Advanced Capitalism*, edited by Pablo Beramendi, Silja Häusermann, Herbert Kitschelt, and Hanspeter Kriesi, 1–40. Cambridge: Cambridge University Press.

Saint-Paul, Gilles. 1996. *Dual Labor Markets: A Macroeconomic Perspective*. Cambridge, MA: MIT Press.

Salehi-Isfahani, Djavad. 2012. "Education, Jobs, and Equity in the Middle East and North Africa." *Comparative Economic Studies* 54(4): 843–861.

Sayigh, Yezid. 2021. "Praetorian Spearhead: The Role of the Military in the Evolution of Egypt's State Capitalism 3.0." 43. MEC Paper Series. London: London School of Economics Middle East Centre.

Schiffbauer, Marc, Hania Sahnoun, and Philip Keefer. 2015. *Jobs or Privileges: Unleashing the Employment Potential of the Middle East and North Africa*. Washington, DC: World Bank.

Schlumberger, Oliver. 2008. "Structural Reform, Economic Order, and Development: Patrimonial Capitalism." *Review of International Political Economy* 15(4): 622–649.

Schmidt, Vivien A. 2009. "Putting the Political Back into Political Economy by Bringing the State Back in Yet Again." *World Politics* 61(3): 516–546.

Schmitter, Philippe C. 1974. "Still the Century of Corporatism?" *The Review of Politics* 36(1): 85–131.

Schmoll, Moritz. 2017. "Broken Promises: The Politics of Lax Enforcement of Tax Laws in Egypt." PhD dissertation, London: London School of Economics.

Schneider, Ben Ross. 2013. *Hierarchical Capitalism in Latin America: Business, Labor, and the Challenges of Equitable Development.* Cambridge: Cambridge University Press.

Schuster, Christian. 2015. "Patrons against Clients: Electoral Uncertainty and Bureaucratic Instability in Patronage States." Draft Paper. London.

Schwedler, Jillian. 2021. Rituals of Protest: CSIS interview. www.csis.org/analysis/rituals-protest.

Sehnbruch, Kirsten, Rocío Méndez Pineda, and Samer Atallah. 2021. "Multidimensional Quality of Employment (QoE) Index in Egypt: The Importance of an Employment Quality Approach to Policy." Cairo: American University of Cairo. https://aps.aucegypt.edu/en/articles/652/policy-paper-multidimensional-quality-of-employment-qoe-index-in-egypt-the-importance-of-an-employment-quality-approach-to-policy.

Seifan, Samir. 2008. "The Reform Paradox in Syria." St Andrews Papers on Contemporary Syria. St Andrews: Centre for Syrian Studies.

Shafiq, M. Najeeb, and Anna Vignoles. 2015. "Beyond the Arab Spring: Education, Earnings, and Protest Participation." Paper presented at *AALIMS–Princeton Conference on Islam and Human Capital.* October.

Simson, Rebecca. 2019. "Africa's Clientelist Budget Policies Revisited: Public Expenditure and Employment in Kenya, Tanzania and Uganda, 1960–2010." *The Economic History Review* 72(4): 1409–1438.

Stewart, Fino, and Juan Yermo. 2009. "Pensions in Africa." 30. OECD Working Papers on Insurance and Private Pensions. Paris: OECD.

Tamirisa, Natalia, and Christoph Duenwald. 2018. *Public Wage Bills in the Middle East and Central Asia.* Washington, DC: International Monetary Fund.

Tansel, Aysit, and Elif Oznur Kan. 2012. "Labor Mobility across the Formal/Informal Divide in Turkey: Evidence from Individual Level Data." *Journal of Economic Studies* 44(4): 617–635.

Tansel, Aysit, and Zeynel Ozdemir. 2014. "Determinants of Transitions across Formal/Informal Sectors in Egypt." MPRA Paper. November 15, 2014. https://mpra.ub.uni-muenchen.de/61183/.

Tell, Tariq. 2013. *The Social and Economic Origins of Monarchy in Jordan.* Springer.

The Economist. 2019a. "Millions of Retiring Arab Civil Servants Need Not Be Replaced." *The Economist*, March 28, 2019.

2019b. "Egypt Is Reforming Its Economy, but Poverty Is Rising." *The Economist*, August 8, 2019.

Thelen, Kathleen. 2014. *Varieties of Liberalization and the New Politics of Social Solidarity.* Cambridge: Cambridge University Press.

Tilly, Charles. 1998. *Durable Inequality.* Berkeley: University of California Press.

Tzannatos, Zafiris, Ishac Diwan, and Joanna Abdel Ahad. 2016. "Rates of Return to Education in Twenty-Two Arab Countries: An Update and Comparison Between MENA and the Rest of the World." 07. ERF Working Papers. Cairo: Economic Research Forum.

Wade, Robert. 2003. *Governing the Market: Economic Theory and the Role of Government in East Asian Industrialization.* Princeton: Princeton University Press.

Wahba, Abdellatif. 2017. "Egypt's Cabinet Approves $2.48 Billion Social Aid Program." *Bloomberg*, May 29, 2017.

Wahba, Jackline. 2009. "Informality in Egypt: A Stepping Stone or a Dead End?" Cairo: Economic Research Forum.

Waldner, David. 1999. *State Building and Late Development.* Ithaca: Cornell University Press.

Walsh, Declan. 2016. "Where's My Mercedes? Egypt's Financial Crisis Hits the Rich." *New York Times*, March 10, 2016.

Walter, Andrew, and Xiaoke Zhang. 2012. *East Asian Capitalism: Diversity, Continuity, and Change.* Oxford: Oxford University Press.

Waterbury, John. 1970. *Commander of the Faithful: The Moroccan Political Elite.* London: Weidenfeld & Nicolson.

1983. *The Egypt of Nasser and Sadat.* Princeton Studies on the Near East. Princeton: Princeton University Press.

Wedeman, Andrew. 2001. "Development and Corruption: The East Asian Paradox." In *Political Business in East Asia*, edited by Edmund Gomez, 50–77. London: Routledge.

Weipert-Fenner, Irene. 2020. "Unemployed Mobilisation in Times of Democratisation: The Union of Unemployed Graduates in Post-Ben Ali Tunisia." *The Journal of North African Studies* 25(1): 53–75.

Weipert-Fenner, Irene, and Jonas Wolff. 2020. *Socioeconomic Protests in MENA and Latin America: Egypt and Tunisia in Interregional Comparison.* New York: Springer.

Werenfels, Isabelle. 2002. "Obstacles to Privatisation of State-owned Industries in Algeria: The Political Economy of a Distributive Conflict." *The Journal of North African Studies* 7(1): 1–28.

Whitehouse, Edward. 2007. *Pensions Panorama: Retirement-Income Systems in 53 Countries*. Paris: OECD.

Willis, Michael. 2012. *Politics and Power in the Maghreb: Algeria, Tunisia and Morocco from Independence to the Arab Spring*. Oxford: Oxford University Press.

Wilson, Rodney J. A. 1988. "Jordan's Trade: Past Performance and Future Prospects." *International Journal of Middle East Studies* 20(3): 325–344.

Woldemichael, Andinet, Margaret Jodlowski, and Abebe Shimeles. 2019. "Labor Market Flexibility and Jobs in Select African Countries." Working Paper 330. African Development Bank.

World Bank. 2008a. "Resolving Jordan's Labor Market Paradox of Concurrent Economic Growth and High Unemployment." 39201-JO. Policy Notes. Washington, DC: World Bank.

2008b. *The Road Not Traveled: Education Reform in the Middle East and North Africa*. Washington, DC: World Bank.

2014. *The Unfinished Revolution: Bringing Opportunity, Good Jobs and Greater Wealth to All Tunisians*. Washington, DC: World Bank.

2018. *The State of Social Safety Nets 2018*. Washington, DC: World Bank.

Yassine, Chaaima. 2015. "The Nature and Determinants of Labor Market Dynamics in the MENA Region." Presented at the ERF Labor and Human Resource Development Meeting, Cairo, July 27.

Zartman, I. William. 1987. *The Political Economy of Morocco*. New York: Praeger.

Acknowledgments

I would like to thank the editors of the Elements series in the Politics of Development, Rachel Beatty Riedl and Ben Ross Schneider, for their great guidance and patience, two anonymous reviewers for their valuable input, and Marion Lieutaud for her outstanding research assistance and data visualization work. I am also grateful to Melani Cammett, Ferdinand Eibl, Ishac Diwan, David Soskice and various colleagues at the LSE for their excellent comments on various versions of my work. I am indebted to the Economic Research Forum in Cairo for making a wide range of labor market datasets available and, critically, for its generous provision of a research grant that allowed me a first investigation of the applicability of "Variety of Capitalism" approaches to the Arab world in 2014–16. Finally, I thank Oxford University Press for permitting me to reuse parts of the following article: Segmented market economies in the Arab world: the political economy of insider-outsider divisions, *Socio-Economic Review*, April 2020 (advance access).

Cambridge Elements ≡

Politics of Development

Rachel Beatty Riedl
Einaudi Center for International Studies and Cornell University

Rachel Beatty Riedl is the Director and John S. Knight Professor of the Einaudi Center for International Studies and Professor in the Government Department and School of Public Policy at Cornell University. Riedl is the author of the award-winning Authoritarian Origins of Democratic Party Systems in Africa (2014) and co-author of From Pews to Politics: Religious Sermons and Political Participation in Africa (with Gwyneth McClendon, 2019). She studies democracy and institutions, governance, authoritarian regime legacies, and religion and politics in Africa. She serves on the Editorial Committee of World Politics and the Editorial Board of African Affairs, Comparative Political Studies, Journal of Democracy, and Africa Spectrum. She is co-host of the podcast Ufahamu Africa.

Ben Ross Schneider
Massachusetts Institute of Technology

Ben Ross Schneider is Ford International Professor of Political Science at MIT and Director of the MIT-Brazil program. Prior to moving to MIT in 2008, he taught at Princeton University and Northwestern University. His books include Business Politics and the State in 20th Century Latin America (2004), Hierarchical Capitalism in Latin America (2013), Designing Industrial Policy in Latin America: Business-Government Relations and the New Developmentalism (2015), and New Order and Progress: Democracy and Development in Brazil (2016). He has also written on topics such as economic reform, democratization, education, labor markets, inequality, and business groups.

Advisory Board

About the Series

The Element series *Politics of Development* provides important contributions on both established and new topics on the politics and political economy of developing countries. A particular priority is to give increased visibility to a dynamic and growing body of social science research that examines the political and social determinants of economic development, as well as the effects of different development models on political and social outcomes.

Cambridge Elements ☰

Politics of Development

Elements in the Series

Developmental States
Stephan Haggard

Coercive Distribution
Michael Albertus, Sofia Fenner and Dan Slater

Participation in Social Policy: Public Health in Comparative Perspective
Tulia G. Falleti and Santiago L. Cunial

Undocumented Nationals
Wendy Hunter

Democracy and Population Health
James W. McGuire

Rethinking the Resource Curse
Benjamin Smith and David Waldner

Greed and Guns: Imperial Origins of the Developing World
Atul Kohli

Everyday Choices: The Role of Competing Authorities and Social Institutions in Politics and Development
Ellen M. Lust

Locked Out of Development: Insiders and Outsiders in Arab Capitalism
Steffen Hertog

A full series listing is available at: www.cambridge.org/EPOD

Printed in the United States
by Baker & Taylor Publisher Services